Project Management Theory 2.0

DR. ABU MOHAMMED FOFANA

Fulton Books, Inc.
Meadville, PA

Published by Fulton Books 2021

ISBN 978-1-63860-355-9 (paperback)
ISBN 978-1-63860-357-3 (digital)

Printed in the United States of America

This book is a synthesis of theoretical and practical knowledge, a dialectic of the true nature of PPGE-based projects. PM Theory 2.0 guides business and project management leaders to lead and prepare employees and teams to manage these complex PM phenomena effectively. If applied fully, PMT 2.0's raison d'etre combined with it's quartet formulation and quintet approaches will salvage complex projects, institutions, and business firms across industries from entropy, disorder and chaos.

Companion Website

Where else do you go to find updates to this book? If you bought this book, you could check for all you need to know including dataset, chapter updates, and more on pmt2.0.globalprojectconsultinggroup. com. *The Project Management Theory 2.0 (PMT 2.0) Simplified Guidebook* will be available on our website. A great discount will be available for all, especially for those of you who have bought *Project Management Theory 2.0.* And if you are interested to learn PM theory from renowned experts, register at projectmanagementsolutionuniversity.com.

The book stemmed from a dissertation research study on Exploring New Theory in the Project Management Field Due to Projectification, Programmification, and Globalization Escalation. Dr. Abu Fofana conducted this study at Northcentral University in partial fulfillment of a Doctor of Philosophy in business administration specializing in project management. Fundamental changes in the PM fields since the submission and defense of the original draft in 2017 have been added, including The Project Management Methodological Selection Intelligence (PMMSI), A Five-Step Approach to managing a complex project, and the predictive Quartet Formulation. The referencing citation style has also changed from the American Psychological Association (APA) to the Chicago Style Manual.

CONTENTS

LIST OF TABLES

LIST OF FIGURES

ABSTRACT

PM is considered the catalyst for worldwide infrastructural development, everyday work organizational format, and a panacea to bureaucracy, lack of productivity, and time mismanagement. PM is estimated to contribute $20.2 trillion USD to the world GDP in 2027. Despite its luring demand, PM's track record remains unabatedly mediocre. PM domain expansion due to PPGE efforts has coalesced temporary and permanent organizational functions, intensified PM's complexity, uncertainty, chaos, nonlinearity, and limited PM theory's ability to describe, explain, and predict in full. The purpose of this multiple-case study was to develop a new PM theory compatible and aligned with what the PM domain has become due to PPGE efforts and to compare the existing and emergent theories. The study gathered data from open-ended online survey questionnaires, seminal works, face-to-face interviews, peer review articles, and archival documents. I selected one hundred and twelve (112) PMP certified professionals from Africa (N = 5), Asia (N = 9), Europe (N =19), Middle East (N = 9), North America (N = 61), and South America (N = 9) from the construction, health care, information technology, education, management, pharmaceutical, and transportation industries to participate in the study. Seven propositions, along with seven questions, were posed. The research study results confirmed the PM domain's enlargement and supported developing PM theory 2.0. The PPGE impact has made it more challenging to complete projects on time, within budget, and without compromising quality. Four key ideations will impact PM theory and practice: PPGE has become the zeitgeist and disruptive innovation. It has manifold infrastructural, governance, theoretical, and management implications. PM training programs should focus on PPGE phenomena. In-depth knowledge of PPGE constructs changes the game between PM mortality and immortality. Good PM theory is significant to PM success.

Acknowledgments

When I began my doctoral research studies at Northcentral University (NCU), which inspired me to write this book, I penned down many goals that I wanted to achieve. I wanted to add significant value to business and project management by helping project and business leaders to fully understand PPGE-based projects and providing them the proper tools they need to manage complex projects most effectively. I also wanted to expand my project management consulting business worldwide. Whether I have achieved what I wanted to become or none, writing these acknowledgments shows that I have come a long way in achieving my goals. But I have never been alone. God has blessed me with encouraging, loving, and generous parents and friends without whom I will have attained none of what I wanted to become. First, I would like to thank my parents, Mohammed Vermunya Nyei-Fofana and Massa Sherif, for instilling a love for education in me. May their souls rest in peace.

Second, a most sincere thank you goes to my friend, Dory Morris, for her unconditional love and support and for sacrificing time to proofread my manuscript. Third, thanks to the NCU staffers, the School of Business and Technology Management, my academic advisors, mentors, and professors for their support, thoughtful advice, and understanding. Fourth, I would like to thank the 112 PM practitioners who voluntarily participated in the research study. I owe immense gratitude to the many strangers who volunteered to propagate the study research flyers on their internet echo chambers. Fifth, it would be remiss if I did not also thank Mohammed Kiawu, Mr. and Mrs. Siaka Sherif, and Mr. and Mrs. Ralph Jimmeh Jr. for the moral support.

CHAPTER 1

Introduction

A good theory describes, explicates, and provides practitioners with the contextual, intellectual, and conceptual underpinnings to make logical predictions. It gives an intervention mechanism or corrective actions concerning project management (PM) phenomena. Its raison d'être explains the who, why, when, how, and where about the phenomena (Ellis and Levy, 2008; Gelso, 2006; Wacker, 1998). The who and what outline the conceptual and theoretical constructs or variables and define the contextual boundaries. Why and how state the purpose and mission of the theory (Gelso, 2006). The constructs or variables must interconnect and interdepend to effectively predict the success and failure and establish a logical internal consistency and reliability. Since a theory operates in a milieu and not in a vacuum, it must be compatible and aligned with its boundary and contextualization. Studies show that a theory that remains infecund and non-heuristic is bound to become stagnant, nebulous, and inutile (Gelso, 2006).

The projectification, programramification, and globalization escalation (PPGE) have transformed the PM domain and expanded its theoretical linchpin beyond its capacity to fully explain, describe, and predict these manifold realities (Godenhjelm, Lundin, and Sjoblom, 2014; Rijke, Herk, Zevenbergen, Ashley, Hertogh, and Heuvelhof, 2014). In 2010, the Project Management Institute (PMI) predicted that the PM sector would create approximately 15.7 million new jobs in every decade due to PPGE efforts (Nasir, Sahibuddin, Ahmad, and Fauzi, 2015). Projectification changes private and public organizations into project-based entities and coalesces the operation of a permanent organization, establishing long-term strategic relationships and alliances with customers, and the implementation of PM's temporary tools and practices (Artto, Valtakoski, and Karki, 2015; Lindsey, Mears, and Cochran, 2016). Programmification integrates program and project portfolio management tasks and PM tactical functions in managing projects and performing semi-permanent or permanent organization functions (Rijke et al., 2014). Godenhjelm et al. (2014) explained that the upsurge in the number of projects that enterprises undertake globally created the need for programmification, an innovative way to manage multiple projects under the auspices of a steady or permanent organization. Project-based organizations (PBOs) integrate an enterprise's management tasks and manage the relationships between project units and their internal and external environments (Kwak, Sadatsafavi, Walewski, and Williams, 2015). Muller et al. (2016) added that PBOs centralize PM activities within the enterprise and balance PM functionalities and its strategic responsibilities. Globalization expands the market horizons, drives innovation, toughens the competition, and increases stakeholders' engagement and interdependencies across borders (Bodislav, Bran, and Iovitu, 2015; Vongprasuth and Choi, 2014). These expansion and convergent efforts have equally augmented the complexity, chaos, uncertainty, and nonlinearity (CCUN) of the PM domain. Unfortunately, the extant PM theory has not kept pace with the emergent, evolutionary, and intricate neologisms dictate.

The literature abounds with descriptions of PM pathologies and taxonomy of project fiascos with little or no discourse on its etiologies. Al-Ahmad et al. (2009) and Johnson et al. (2015) outlined over fifty project failures and identified theories developed to serve as panaceas to PM doldrums. Moreover, the International Project Management Association, the Project Management Institute, the Association for Project Management, and the French Project Management Association, to name a few examples, continue to establish standards, methodologies, models, and tools to improve PM mortality rate or sustainable success. PMI, for instance, has proposed the Organizational Project Maturity Model (OPM3) to enhance maturity in managing complex projects (Alami, Bouksour, and Beidouri, 2015). Irrespective of these rescue efforts, the rate of project mortality or failure remains unabated. Boston's Big Dig project sustained an $11.8 billion cost overrun (Fein, 2012). PMI averred that businesses lose an average of $122 million for every $ billion investment that they make in PM (Project Management Institute [PMI], 2014). Swanson and Chermack (2013) explained that a theory could negatively or positively impact an organization or a society. Studies indicate that when a theory and practice are reciprocal and aligned, the synergy produces positive results (Herbert, Guadiano, and Forma, 2013). A fissure, therefore, exists between PM current theory and what PM domain has become due to PPGE (Wilkinson, Smallidge, Boyd, and Giblin, 2015).

Bergman et al. (2013) and Maranon and Pera (2015) called for developing a new PM theory that will defrag these neologisms and establish internal consistency among them. Besteiro et al. (2015), Kuura et al. (2013), Mir and Pinnington (2014), and Oellgaard (2013) argued that PM theory is narrow and could not describe, explain, and predict complex, nonlinear, and uncertain realities. Almeida and Soares (2014) and Sternberg (2016) indicated that, due to the reductionist or microcosmic understanding of PM phenomena, the rate of project completion has stifled. Kuura et al. (2013) argued that the PM field has no theory. Its theory development is still working in progress. Ferrero (2015), Park and Kang (2008), and Sauchelli (2013) indicated that lack of understanding of the PM domain due to PPGE efforts makes a project and the achievement of its objective susceptible to mortality (failure). Mitchell and Schmitz (2013) and Wray (2015) scathingly heaped criticism on the current PM theory for its limited capacity to fully describe, explicate, and accurately predict PM phenomena success and failure because of PPGE.

Background

In the 1980s, PM theories, tools, and techniques began widespread use in industries. However, the presence of immortal construction projects such as the Great Pyramid of Giza in Egypt, the

Parthenon, and the Acropolis Museum in Greece, and the Colosseum of the Roman Empire, to name a few examples, signified that formal or informal PM practices, models, and methods did exist in ancient times (Garel, 2012; Kwak, 2005; Seymour and Hussein, 2014).

Contrary to the claim that PM theory then was elusive, a keen look at the Acropolis Museum and the caryatids that support its entablature, for instance, also indicated meticulous and professional execution of theory into practice (Kwak et al., 2015). Moreover, the development of critical path method (CPM) and program evaluation review technique (PERT), the Gantt Chart, research and development (RandD), earned value management (EVM), and the work breakdown structure (WBS) contributed immensely to PM theory, methodology, and techniques. The National Aeronautics and Space Administration, the Department of Defense, and other federal organizations used these proven techniques, one way or another, to design and implement sophisticated, engineering, and technological landmark projects such as the Polaris project (1956–1961), the Manhattan project (1942–1945), and the Apollo Project (1969 -1972) (Chiu, 2010).

The exponential growth of public and private projects the world has over decades continued to deteriorate, making it harder for projects to achieve immortality or sustainability (McCurdy, 2013). The ubiquity of globalization through technological advancement and the liberalization of trade among nations has posed grave organizational success challenges. As projects' mortality rates increased, the need to projectify and programify public and private projects spurred increasing interest; most organizations viewed projectification and programmification as catalysts that bring about sustainable competitive advantage.

Statement of the Problem

PPGE has broadened the PM domain's scope beyond its theoretical capacity to accurately explain, describe, and predict phenomena (Ramazani et al., 2014; Svejvig and Andersen, 2014). Studies show PM temporality connotes projects' disengagement from their environments (Hanisch and Wald, 2012). PPGE transforms organizations into project-based and interdisciplinary entities, functioning within the PM and organizational contexts (Artto et al., 2015; Godenhjelm et al., 2014). Globalization enhances opportunities and risks (Bodislav et al., 2015; Vongprasuth and Choi, 2014). Godenhjelm et al. (2014) argued that PPGE increases a project's environmental, political, and entrepreneurial constructs and complexities. Padalkar and Gopinath (2016) and Yung (2015) reported that irrespective of the plethora of literature written about PM, its theory is incoherent and partial. PM theory's failure to keep pace with the realities and challenges of these emergent and intricate neologisms has created an epistemological gap between the current PM theory and what the PM domain has become due to PPGE (Bergman et al., 2013; Maranon and Pera, 2015). This hiatus has added to the litany of PM's pathologies. Over 60 percent of megaprojects fail (Fein, 2012). Worldwide annual investment in PM falls between $6 to $9 trillion (Flyvbjerg, 2014). In a decade, an estimate of Asian infrastructure expansion projects will reach $8 trillion (Lu et al., 2015). Sternberg (2016) suggested that most PM practitioners view PM phenomena from a reductionist or instrumentalist perspective due to PM theoretically narrow vista. Ahern et al. (2013) showed that the PM theoretical foundation is in decline; it cannot fully describe, explain, and predict complex projects' success or failure.

Purpose of the Study

The purpose of this multiple-case study was twofold: to develop a new PM theory 2.0 (PMT2.0) that will be compatible to and aligned with what the PM domain has become due to PPGE, and to explore and compare the extant PM theory and the PMT2.0. The study organized, analyzed, and compared empirical evidence or data gathered from interviews, strategic organizational reports, and archives. The multiple data sources made it reliable to determine if PPGE had expanded the PM theoretical base beyond its capacity to describe fully, explain, and predict complex PM phenomena. It also determined whether a fissure existed between PM current theory and what PM domain had become due to PPGE efforts, and which theory (the extant PM or the emergent PMT2.0) was superior (Wilkinson, Smallidge, Boyd, and Giblin, 2015).

The research purposively recruited 112 participants from the construction, education, health care, IT, management, pharmaceutical, and transportation industries. About 90 percent completed the online open-ended interview questions, and the remaining 10 percent had phone or face-to-face interviews conducted mainly in the North American region. The study was conducted in the United States of America. The population sample was primarily limited to PM practitioners, including PMI chapters across North America, Europe, Asia Pacific, the Middle East, Africa, and Latin America. Participating units comprised autonomous project management offices or teams operating in an outsource and PPGE-based organization, both private and public. ATLAS.ti 8 software managed and analyzed data accurately.

Theoretical/Conceptual Framework

Due to PPGE's effects, PM's temporality concept is no longer tenable in most project management milieus. Besides, the canonical application of PM's lifecycle phraseology (initiation, planning, implementation or execution, and closing) and a focus on its triple constraints have imperceptibly waned and lost universal acclaim. Today, projects are managed within or in association with permanent or semi-permanent organizations executing PM-proven concepts and concomitantly performing the mundane business or organizational functions (Artto et al., 2015; Lindsey et al., 2016). A globalized project-based organization also requires a web of networking and interconnected stakeholders located across numerous frontiers. This makes understanding PM's current domain's philosophical or theoretical basis arduous but imperative (Bodislav et al., 2015; Vongprasuth and Choi, 2014).

Since business management and PM fields are practical disciplines, a good and virtuous theory must demonstrate real-life application in addressing these challenges and meet the criteria of the four essential theoretical elements. These factors include a clear definition and description of the phenomena in question, identification of its domain and boundary, the establishment of relationships among its constructs and variables, and predictive capability of events that may impact a project's mortality or immortality (Naor et al., 2013) (see Figure 1). The Theory of Constraints (TOC) and the Stakeholder Theory (ST) have adhered to the criteria of sound theory and provided relevant theoretical underpinnings to the field of business in general and particularly to PM's state of affairs.

Theory of Constraints (TOC)

TOC owes its provenance to Eli Goldratt. In 1984, he introduced and advocated TOC. Central to TOC is the idea that constraints (physical resources, market uncertainties, and regulatory issues) are coterminous to entrepreneurial undertakings (Simsit et al. 2014), (Naor et al., 2013).

To sustain a competitive posture, business leaders must continually identify, exploit, subordinate, elevate, and repeat (the removal of) the constraints until the business had achieved sustainability

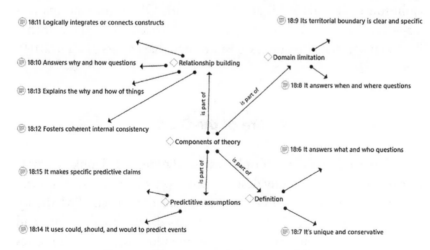

Figure 1. Basic essential elements of theory

(Simsit et al., 2014). The TOC helps manage complex, uncertain, and chaotic PM phenomena, including project risk, cost management schedule, monitor, and control (Steyn, 2000, 2001). While TOC has claimed the approbation of most scholars and theoreticians, Bevilacqua et al. (2009), Johnson et al. (2015) criticized TOC for the uncertainty in buffer time management.

Stakeholder Theory (ST)

Although Adolf A. Berle conceived the ST concept in 1931 (Flak and Nordheim, 2016; Berle, 1931), Thomas Freeman popularized it in 1984 (Littau et al., 2010). ST has been widely extolled in the PM milieus due to its specific emphasis on the significant role stakeholders play in business or PM management; their buy-in and engagement are integral to any project's sustainability. Furthermore, due to the multiplicity and diversity of stakeholders' vested interests in the PPGE-based project environment, ST's importance cannot be overstated. Studies show that an essential part of project immortality depends on the extent to which stakeholders' disparate social, legal, cultural, economic, and environmental interests are managed with the respect, honesty, fairness, and sensibility that they deserve (Johnson et al., 2015; Littau et al., 2010). Often immoral managers—Ken Lay, Bernie Ebbers, Dennis Kozlowski, and others of that ilk—manage stakeholders as costs rather than assets (Patra, 2010; Sweeney, 2002).

Nature of the Study

The study used a multiple-case study method. Unlike a single case or a holistic case study design, a multiple-case study method can explore the impact of PPGE and compare the current PM theory and the proposed PMT 2.0. It also focused on gathering data and comparing those data from disparate units located in multiple sites (Yin, 2009, 2014). It employed various research instruments such as documentation, archival records, interviews, direct and indirect participant observation, and physical artifacts to gather data from participants. To fully achieve the research study objective, the propositions and research questions were inextricably linked. Studies show that data collected from an assortment of research instruments makes replication, triangulation, generalizability, reliability, and quality control a reality, a goal that the application of multiple case study methods will realize (Yin, 2014).

Scholars and theorists agree that multiple-case study methodology is appropriate for theory generating, developing, and testing (Harlow, 2010; Yin, 2014); It is adaptable to organizations' changes. A single study design mainly concentrates on a unit of analysis conducted primarily on one country (Miterev et al., 2016). A holistic design lacks specificity and is designed to handle universal or general units of analysis (Yin, 2009, 2014).

About 101 participants completed the online open-ended questions. Only 11 participants from the North American region had a face-to-face or phone interview. Studies show that open-end questions empower research participants to fully express their points of view (Yin, 2009, 2014). There were PPGE-based units (N =56). Eight (8) units were selected from each of seven industries: construction, transportation, health care, IT, pharmaceutical, education, and management (Eriksson and Kovalainen, 2012). Equally, PM practitioners (N = 56) were selected from various International Project Management Association (IPMA) associated member-based geographic regions. There were eight units from North America, eight from South America, eight from Europe, eight from the Asia Pacific, and eight from Africa. The geographic dispersion of the sample increased the generalizability of the research. The ages of participants and their years of experience were at least 24 and sixth months, respectively. ATLAS.ti software was used to sort, categorize, code, and identify patterns, similarities, and dissimilarities among empirical evidence or data pieces. This reduced rooted out errors and enhanced the results' quality, credibility, and trustworthiness. The research ensured an interview restage aimed to follow up and clarify conflicting and ambiguous statements and test the reliability of data before synthesizing and reporting results (Padgett, 2004). The study launched a pilot case study to test equipment and apply the research protocol encompassing procedures, methods, and ethics (Yin, 2009, 2014).

Participants' autonomy, as well as the protection of their data, was guaranteed. Alphanumeric or letter codes such as unit1-agent1 and unit2-agent2, to name a few examples, were implemented to conceal their identities. Besides emails and other self-completion questionnaires, the study used web-based sites such as SurveyMoneky.com and Google Survey to coordinate and structure questionnaires to the specific and targeted populations mentioned supra. Participants' permission was required or given before the official commencement of online and onsite surveys, interviews, and any other contact with participants. Surveys and interview questions were mainly based on open-ended questions.

Research Questions

The research questions focused on obtaining from participants, PM practitioners, and PPGE-based units, empirical data required to achieve the purpose of developing a new PM theory 2.0 (PMT2.0). PMT 2.0 is intended to be compatible with and aligned with the PM domain spectrum, including the impact of PPGE, and explore the similarities and dissimilarities between the extant PM theory and the PMT2.0. The study endeavored to seek answers from participants, literature reviews, seminal works, and archival documents to the following questions:

RQ1. How do PPGE efforts broaden the scope of the PM domain and impact the application of PM theory?

RQ2. How do PPGE efforts limit the current PM theory's capacity to fully describe, explain, and predict complex, uncertain, and nonlinear phenomena?

RQ3. How do a complete understanding, description, and prediction of complex, uncertain, and nonlinear phenomena impact a project's success?

RQ4. How do PPGE efforts transform the PM domain and its theory?

RQ5. How do these transformational efforts impact or influence PM theory and practice?

RQ6. How does the development of new PM theory (the proposed PMT 2.0, for example) eliminate the gap between PM extant theory and the expansion of the project management domain due to PPGE?

RQ7. What challenges have PM practitioners experienced due to PPGE efforts?

Significance of the Study

As its nomenclature indicates, PM manages the construction and development of infrastructures that transform organizations and communities. The Brooklyn Bridge, Boston's Big Dig, the Eiffel Tower, and O'Hare International Airport are cases in point (Dimitri, 2013; Sternberg, 2016; Thamhain, 2014). Lindsey et al. (2016) explained that public and private organizations adapt to projectification or programmification because they breed innovative solutions to complex and nonlinear situations. They also increase efficiency and public support and reduce cost. Nations spend approximately $9 trillion every year on big projects, approximately 8 percent of their gross domestic product (GDP) (Flyvbjerg, 2014). The United States National Academy of Public Administration [The Academy] (2015) plans to apply the time-tested project management and program management tools to manage programs incredibly complex programs. The Academy believes that well-trained PM professionals can manage a complex project in the most cost-effective and administratively effective manner; programmification has demonstrated successes across various industries and organizations. It has been estimated that the Fed will save over $995 billion by 2025 through programmification and projectification efforts. In a decade, an estimate of Asian infrastructure expansion projects is expected to surpass $8 trillion (Lu et al., 2015).

Despite these mammoth investments in PM endeavors, PM stakeholders receive only a fraction of their investment returns. Charrett and Loots (2015) and Ramazani and Jergeas (2014) indicated that approximately 65–68 percent of megaprojects fail. Proposed remedies to the high rate of project mortality are perfunctory and inadequate (Alami et al., 2015). The literature review points to the current PM theoretical foundation as a culprit; it has not fully described, explained, and predicted what the field of project management has become because of PPGE expansion efforts (Boardman, Vining, and Weimer, 2016). PM theoretical foundation propagates linear and deterministic approaches to solve these complex, chaotic, uncertain, and nonlinear phenomena. Swanson and Chermack (2013) explained that a theory could negatively or positively impact an organization or a society. To sustain a realistic outcome from translating theory into practice depends on the compatibility between the theory and phenomena it describes, explains, and predicts (Wilkinson et al., 2015). Studies also show that when theory and practice are aligned and compatible, they produce tangible and satisfactory outcomes (Herbert et al., 2013).

The exploration of new theory development, the proposed PMT 2.0, is intended to contribute to the PM field in two ways: to provide PM practitioners with a complete description and explanation of the PM field's related constructs because of PPGE. It will also undergird practitioners with a coordinated system of knowledge and interdependent and logical constructs, the application of which will help PM practitioners predict the mortality and immortality of complex, uncertain, nonlinear, and chaotic project phenomena.

Definition of Key Terms

Escalation. The Advanced English Dictionary defines escalation as increasing, expanding, intensifying, or enlarging something.

Globalization. Globalization is the act of changing an organization from a local to an internationally based entity. It increases risks and opportunities (Bodislav et al., 2015).

Macrocosm and microcosm. Microcosm is a metaphor used here to mean a unit of a complex social system, or a part of an entire project (macrocosm) (Strosetzki, 2014).

Management Functions. Management of an organization or a business enterprise generally plans, organizes, leads, and controls scarce capital, material, and human resources to accomplish business or organizational objectives (Kuura et al., 2013).

Mortality and immortality. Mortality means failure, termination, or closure. The opposite is immortality which means sustainable success (Ferrero, 2015).

Phenomenon/phenomena. A phenomenon is a notable occurrence in the PM field due to PPGE. It also means complex and uncertain realities (phenomena).

Project Management Institute (PMI). PMI is a nonprofit organization that develops standards, conducts educational research, trains, and provides a web of networking channels and opportunities to its chapter members (Lock, 2013).

Programmification. Programmification is a formal process established to change an existing organization's structure to manage a group of programs along with or under the control of a permanent organization (Patanakul, 2011; Rijke et al., 2014).

Project Portfolio Management (PPM). PPM handles a mix of projects, programs, and subprojects. It ensures the effective use of resources (Kaiser et al., 2014)

Project-based organizations (PBOs). PBOs combine enterprise and project management standards to deliver services more efficiently and expeditiously (Artto et al., 2015).

Projectification. Projectification is a formal act of changing an organization's structure to perform regular organizational functions and PM functions (Artto et al., 2015; Maylor et al., 2006).

Sustainability. Sustainability connotes success, profitability, maximization of return on capital, competitive advantage, and complete customer satisfaction that endure (Maltzman and Shirley, 2010).

Summary

PM's current theory has not expanded its domain, considering project management's growth and expansion due to PPGE efforts (Godenhjelm et al., 2014; Rijke et al., 2014). PPGE-based organizations integrate disparate management functionalities: business management and project management (Artto et al., 2015; Lindsey et al., 2016). Anthropoulos et al. (2015), Batkins and Brannon (2014), Boardman et al. (2016), and Venkatesh et al. (2014) stated that managing project-based, program-based, and global-based organizations is complex, uncertain, nonlinear, and chaotic. Studies also noted the epistemological fissure between the current PM theory and the PM field's expansion due to these new manifold constructs. PMT 2.0 can provide a complete explanation, description, and prediction of these phenomena. It also embodies a knowledge system that makes PM practitioners feasible to predict projects' mortality and immortality across industries. The research used a multiple-case in gathering or collecting data from PM-based units and practitioners from multiple sites or locations (Yin, 2009, 2014).

CHAPTER 2

Literature Review

The purpose of this multiple-case study was twofold: to develop a new PM theory 2.0 (PMT2.0) and to explore the similarities and dissimilarities between the extant PM theory and the emergent PMT2.0. Data gathered from observations, interviews, strategic organization reports, and archives were compared to determine whether PPGE had expanded the PM domain's theoretical base, whether PPGE affects PM success, and which theory (the extant or the new) was superior. The study was held in the United States of America.

Key terms, themes, or constructs that directly or indirectly impact PM field of study, PM theory, project complexity, mortality, and immortality included projectification, programmification, project-based organization, and globalization. The population sample was limited to PMI chapter members across the globe. Participating units comprised autonomous project management offices or teams operating in an outsource and project-based organization, both private and public. ATLAS.ti 8 was employed to organize, manage, and analyze data better and make network diagrams.

The study organized the literature review into the following categories: (a) documentation, (b) definition of theory, (c) philosophical views of PM Theory, (d) PM theoretical domain expansion, (e) the quandary of PM/IT Methodologies, (f) the paradox of integrating temporality and permanence, (g) PMT 2.0 theoretical foundation, (h) comparison between PM theory and PMT 2.0, (i) the theory of PMT 2.0, (j) the application and praxis of PM theory, (k) the application of research methods in theory development, and (l) the impact of PPGE on critical industries.

Documentation

The writing of this literature review required the reading or consulting of various categories of literature, including but not limited to seminal works, theoretical articles, peer review and scholarly journals, articles written about issues and debates, key findings, and research designs. The study used databases and search engines to obtain the needed information to achieve the research purpose and objective. Most of the databases are located at Northcentral University Library. The search engines and databases included Roadrunner, SAGE, EBSCOhost, ProQuest, Business Source Complete, ebrary, RefWorks, IEEE Xplore, ScienceDirect, and SpringerLink. The study also used Google Scholar and Google Books engines to search for peer-reviewed scholarly journals and seminal works.

The writing of key words theory, project management, project, projectification, globalization, programmification, program, project portfolio, and project-based organization in the search engines generated peer-reviewed journals and a wide array of other information. These data shed light on theory development, including its four theoretical criteria and those of a good theory's virtues. Other search terms included International Project Management Association, Project Management Institute, Association for Project Management, French Project Management Association, Prince2, PMBOK, international projects, complex projects, and megaprojects.

Definition of Theory

The theory has no universally unique definition. Philosophers, theorists, and scholars hold disparate ontological, epistemological, and methodological points of view about it (Creswell, 2003,

2014). Most theorists, however, agreed that good theory must be able to clearly define phenomena and domain, create relationships, and predict events between variables. Gelso (2006) and Wacker (1998, 2004) further indicated that theory must meet the four theoretical elements' criteria and the eight virtues of a good theory to stand out. The four elements are conceptual definition, domain limitations, relationship-building, and predictive capabilities (Wacker, 1998, 2004). The eight criteria are as follows: uniqueness, parsimony, conservatism, generalizability, fecundity, internal consistency, empirical riskiness, and abstraction (Gelso, 2006; Wacker, 1998, 2004) (see Appendix J). Wacker (1998) explained that a theory could not be distinguishable from practice and must answer the who, what, when, how, why, should, could, and would questions about phenomena. Gelso (2006) indicated that a theory could be a formal or informal, objective or subjective, and realistic or idealistic relationship that implicitly exists among theoretical constructs. Harlow (2009, 2010) explained that a theory provides order and understanding of phenomena like the laws of the natural sciences. Byron and Thatcher (2016) defined theory as a means that explains a phenomenon and how it works in a specific situation. Herbert et al. (2013) defined theory as a set of concepts, principles, and statements that describe the interaction among constructs and can describe, predict, and guide interventions in certain situations.

Lalonde et al. (2010) explained that PM theory deepens practitioners' and researchers' understanding of project management's epistemological issues. They indicated that PM theory's epistemological issue could be practical (heuristic), quantitative, qualitative, and reflective (qualitative and pragmatic). A heuristic discipline is mainly concerned with PM's functional aspects, like what practitioners do daily in managing projects. Swanson and Chermack (2013) classified theories as local, midrange, and grand. Local, or minitheories, have limited boundaries, whereas midrange boundaries give a larger perspective of phenomena. Grand theories' boundaries are more comprehensive than the limitations of minitheories and midrange theories and are, therefore, more generalizable.

Philosophical Views of PM Theory

The number of philosophers, advocates, theoretical proponents, and thinkers that have persuaded, influenced, and undergirded PM's theoretical foundation is infinite. Salient among the most influential thinkers are the reductionists, instrumentalists, realists, and idealists (Stam, 1996, 2000). They also make worldly predictions about events and produce healthy scientific debate on what theory is and how it can be applied to practical situations (Stam 1996, 2000).

Reductionists believe that realities or phenomena are best understood by breaking them into chunks and examining their components separately (Stam, 1996, 2000). Concepts and approaches. such as the work breakdown structure (WBS), earned value management (EVM), critical path method (CPM), and program evaluation procedure technique (PERT), are reductionist implements (Project Management Institute [PMBOK Guide], 2013). An accurate description and understanding of phenomena without reducing them into parts is illusory to reductionists. This is diametric to complexity theory and idealism, describing and explicating complex realities from a holistic perspective (Stam, 2000). The caveat is that humans are not materials. It is implausible to reduce cultures, faith, and behaviors into microscopic objects or other monism forms.

Instrumentalists consider theories to be tools used to understand and solve practical problems. These may include maximizing the return on investment and enhancing short-term or quarterly earnings performance rather than long-term profitability or sustainable growth. What matters to the instrumentalists is the end value.

The theory of realism espouses a dualistic view about phenomena, namely that a phenomenon is real but exists autonomously outside of our perception and thought. On the other hand, the idealists believe actual knowledge about phenomena comes from what the mind constructs or the meanings it provides (O'Leary, 2007; Turpin, 2015). Ryan (2015) averred that our epistemological understanding and sense-experience of phenomena is the only thing that is real (Caro, 2015; Sullivan, 2009). These theoretical thoughts can metaphorically be further divided into two philosophical persuasions, namely microcosm and macrocosm. The microcosmists consist of reductionists and instrumentalists. Quantitative research inquiry is their basis for seeking knowledge about PM phenomena. On the other hand, macrocosmists consist of idealists. They apply qualitative research methodology to understand PM realities.

Microcosm. Classical project management theory describes phenomena as linear and deterministic, i.e., there are always cause-and-effect relationships between one thing and another. PM concepts such as a trilogy, the focus on a project's scope, cost, and schedule exemplify this ethos (Gransberg et al., 2013). Besteiro et al. (2015), Gransberg et al. (2013), Mir and Pinnington (2014), and Oellgaard (2013) explained that project management theory could not handle complex realities. Consequently, and despite enormous investment in managing megaprojects, approximately 65–68 percent of megaprojects fail (Charrett and Loots, 2015; Ramazani and Jergeas 2014). Padalkar and Gopinath (2015) agreed that projects' continued failure gave rise to project portfolio management.

Sternberg (2016) suggested that due to the inability of microcosmic or reductionist views of project management, conflict, resistance, ontological, and epistemological incompatibilities, and a lack of preparation to handle the known and the unknown unknowns continue, unabated, to stymie the rate of project immortality. The literature is replete with criticisms that connoisseurs and practitioners have continually heaped on this ethos for its limited capacity to effectively handle complex and nonlinear realities.

Macrocosm. The study's project management field's emergence as a macrocosmic of phenomena is antithetical to the static, technocratic, prescriptive, and microcosmic views. Macrocosmists view project management phenomena as holistic, nonlinear, complex, adaptive, uncertain, and beyond microcosmic thinkers' capability to understand, let alone manage, in a sustainable fashion. The plethora of project management malaise archived in the literature due to the current PM theoretical foundations' limitation is a case in point.

No doubt, PPGE has broadened the PM concept, context, and theoretical domain, making the current PM mindset unable to solve new and complex realities fully. Rijke et al. (2014) highlighted the distinction between project-oriented tasks and strategic program management projects. They explained that while program-mification handles different and long-duration projects, programs, and sub-projects simultaneously, project management focuses on achieving functions that have a short period to deliver or complete its objectives. Miterev et al. (2015) indicated that a particular type of program requires a set of different competencies. Brookes et al. (2014) suggested investing and prioritizing long-term goals and attaining a project management maturity level. Godenhjelm et al. (2014) indicated that projectification has significantly changed the public and private sectors' structures.

Bergman et al. (2013) outlined the effect of projectification as dualistic: an ancillary (outsourcing) of or the integration of out-sourcing and strategic insourcing operations into the enterprise. They proposed that success in expanding the project management field through projectification depended on product, process, people, and structure. Lu et al. (2014) indicated that the tasks involved in managing megaprojects are manifold and have become intractable to measure. They noted that there was a relationship between proj-ect complexity and hidden workload. They, therefore, developed a ProjectSim software to analyze the complexity of megaprojects using the 2010 Shanghai project as a case study. Flyvbjerg (2014) high-lights managing megaprojects' complexity, risks, cost overruns, over-stressed schedules, and quality minimization.

Moreover, Schmidt (2016) and Subramanian (2013) stated that a theory's ultimate obligation is to fulfill its intended raison d'etre to achieve what is suitable and valuable for organizations. Schmidt (2016) also noted that a proper understanding of phenomena mat-ters; it helps direct, integrate, and control interactions within the natural world. The instrumentalists claim that a business enterprise's purpose is to maximize shareholder return on investment (Ofori et al., 2014). Idealists describe and explicate complex realities from a holis-tic perspective instead of reductionism (Stam, 2000). Besteiro et al. (2015), Mir and Pinnington (2014), and Oellgaard (2013) explained that project management theory could not handle complex realities. Sternberg (2016) suggested that due to the narrow view from which microcosmists understand the truth about phenomena, the rate of project completion has stifled in the project management field.

PM's macrocosmist theory is a direct reaction to the static, prescriptive, and microcosmic view. The emergence of projectification and programmification has further intensified and broadened the project management domain's complexity and nonlinearity. Packendorf and Lindgren (2013) described these new trends as transformative, restructuring, and multifaceted; they have changed traditional projects' structure to project-based and strategic management organizations that operate permanently. Brookes et al. (2014) suggested investing and prioritizing long-term goals and attaining a project management maturity level to better understand the knowledge gap due to these expansion efforts. Godenhjelm et al. (2014) indicated that projectification has significantly changed the public and private sectors' structures.

PM Theoretical Domain Expansion Due to PPGE

PPGE has profoundly impacted PM theoretical foundation, organizational culture, and its structure in three discernable ways: (a) it changes PM domain and raison d'etre, (b) it increases the complexity of the PM domain and its modus operandi, and (c) it creates a mismatch between theory and phenomena.

How PPGE changes PM domain and raison d'etre.

Midler (1995), the proponent of projectification, indicated that projectification incorporates aspects of a permanent organization and retains PM's temporal nature in a parallel fashion. Also, while the PM domain has increased, its theoretical boundary remains unaltered. Battistuzzo and Piscopo (2015) and Trkman (2010) explained that PPGE expands the endogenous and exogenous risks and challenges of international projects. The changes that PPGE brings about impact PM's domain significantly, making the field nonlinear and impervious to prescriptive, deterministic, and linear solutions. Boardman and Weimer (2016) noted that programmification changes managerial efficiency and productivity both in the short and long terms.

Programmification attempts to structure, coordinate, and manage interrelated and independent projects or subprojects with different objectives aligned with a firm's strategic goal. Arvidsson (2009) indicated that applying concepts such as time, task, team, and transition creates a profound difference between permanent and temporary functions. Studies show that scramble disruptions can occur when a project continues to separately maintain its short-term goal instead of pursuing an enterprise's long-term objective (San Cristóbal, 2015). Soderlund and Muller (2014) indicated the complex nature of the London 2012 Olympics and the Heathrow Terminal 5 projects, for instance, was a base of failure to achieve cost, time, and quality objectives.

Arvidsson (2009) asserted that an understanding of PM temporal function's coexistence and permanent organizational operation improves PM performance. Jerbrant (2013) and Johnson et al. (2016) warned that unless a new theory is developed to explain the knowledge gap between the PM discipline and recent advancements in the PM field, success in managing projects will continue to dwindle. What is defined as a temporal undertaking to accomplish a product and service can now take on permanent endeavors and produce results without regard to a project lifecycle. In other words, PM's objective is no longer limited to a temporary, unique, pre-determined, and homogenous endeavor; it is geared toward accomplishing multiple goals (Oerlemans and Pretorius, 2014). Rigby et al. (2014) explained that PPGE exacerbates PM policymaking gridlock, bureaucracy, and resistance. It is complex, arduous, and requires forethought and a deep understanding of the interconnectivity and dynamism among stakeholders across borders.

Beset by the continual failure of PM's prescriptive management system, He et al. (2014) introduced a complex theoretical framework that explained and predicted outcomes that involved technological, organizational, goal, environmental, cultural, and information complexities. The world of project management is diverse, complex, incompatible, and uncertain. Moreover, unlike PM extant theory,

PMT2.0 will describe phenomena as pervasive; it is hard to establish deterministically or cause-and-effect relationships between constructs; variations among constructs are not linear and predictable (Bland and Roberts-Pittman, 2014).

Majoor (2016) outlined ethnographic effects on complex projects such as economic, political, and the plethora of stakeholders to achieve success. Pitsis, Shankaran, Gudergan, and Clegg (2014) indicated that the emergence of globalization, projectification, and programmification had created a new conceptualization that can underpin the complexity of managing PPGE-based organizations characterized by various tasks, unpredictable events, and nonlinear activities. Cudworth and Hobden (2012) indicated that, like complexity theory, PMT 2.0 would make a viable theoretical foundation for project management; through projectification, programmification, and globalization, managing projects has become a complex and unpredictable phenomenon.

The application of complexity theory is a relevant foundation for a better understanding of phenomena; it is contingent upon and susceptible to criticism and refutation but provides profound epistemological perceptions of the universe and uncertainties that it contains. Johnson et al. (2015) and Kim and Wilemon (2013) indicated that complexity theory provides project management practitioners intellectual and practical understanding of the complex world's intricacies. Complex projects are hard to perform even if experts manage them; there are numerous components and layers of conditions or decisions required to make them work. Interference of known unknowns and unknown unknowns is always probable (Gransberg et al., 2013).

How PPGE increases the complexity of PM domain and modus operandi

The integration of PPGE has expanded the PM domain. Kwak et al. (2015) and Kuura et al. (2013) indicated that projectification performs dual roles: it provides guidance, support, and oversight and, at the same time, performs an enterprise's operational functions of managing relationships between project units and their internal and external environments. Oerlemans and Pretorius (2014) pointed out PPGE has pervaded sundry academic fields, including organizational sciences and projects across industries. These include inter-organizations, megaprojects, and joint ventures, to name a few. Moreover, because of PPGE, the project management field has shifted gears from a mere emphasis on a project's scope, time, and cost to apply a holistic approach to managing projects.

Gallo (2012) showed that an essential key element of complexity theory is the convergence of manifold stakeholders' concerns across multiple jurisdictions. He explained that the complex system is not a defined theoretical boundary; it is a set of social constructs and interactions of multivariate dimensions. He suggested that to optimize sustainable business success, project management practitioners must shift from applying prescriptive and predefined conceptualization to an autopoietic, adaptive, and emergence paradigm, from a closed system to an open one and linear to the nonlinear ethos of project management phenomena (Gallo, 2012). Pinto, Novaska, Antholon, and Besteiro (2014) indicated that having a complete understanding of the relationships among the manifold variables or constructs could determine the level of internal consistency and reliability. They suggested that PMBOK Guide, theory, and method have failed to focus on these complexities. Ahern et al. (2013) showed that the PM theoretical foundation is in decline. It cannot fully describe, explain, and predict the nonlinear and interdependent relationships among complex projects across industries. In other words, the current prescriptive management approaches cannot predict the unpredictable unknowns and the unknown unknowns in managing complex projects. This hiatus has added to the litany of PM pathologies. Approximately 60 percent of worldwide annual investment in projects fails (Flyvbjerg, 2014). Sternberg (2016) suggested that due to PM theoretical narrow vista, most PM practitioners equally view PM phenomena from a reductionist or silo perspective. Pinto et al. (2014) indicated that having a complete understanding of the various constructs' relationships can determine the level of internal consistency and reliability.

A mismatch between PM Theory and PM Phenomena

Understanding who, why, when, how, and where about PM phenomena are required in developing a good and genuine theory. The "who" and "what," for example, define the theory's constituents, constructs, or variables. The "when" and "how" determine the theoretical boundaries. "Why" and "how" define the theory's mission and the reason for its existence. When the who and what category does not adequately describe the phenomena of interest, a practical application (PA) of the theory becomes complicated.

Moreover, when the "why" and "how" category has a mission creep or mission enlargement, the theory's power of internal consistency wanes. This makes the translation of theory to PA unrealistic, if not impossible (Gerow et al., 2015). This theoretical mission creep metaphor has befallen the PM discipline for decades.

Through PPGE efforts, the scope of project management (PM) has expanded, spanning across a plethora of industries and borders (Godenhjelm et al., 2014; Miterev et al., 2015; Packendorf and Lindgren, 2013; Rijke et al., 2014; Vongprasuth and Choi, 2014). These expansion and amalgamation efforts have equally enlarged the PM domain. Unfortunately, PM's current theory remains inert or ossified and has not kept pace with these novels' dictates and intricately challenging phenomena.

The choice of a theory is essential. An evaluation of a project's performance based on reductionist criteria, for instance, will produce outcomes that are narrow and will not reflect on the whole system (Gallo, 2012). Besides, incompatibility relating to a phenomenon, how we can learn it, and what method we can use to understand it can constrain the translation of theory into a practical application.

The PM theoretical knowledge is rooted in reductionism, instrumentalism, and realism. Reductionists carry the notion that the surefire way to have a detailed understanding of reality is to divide it into parts. On the other hand, instrumentalists believe a theory's primary end value is to maximize a business's profitability (Mitchell and Schmitz, 2013; Schmidt, 2016; Stam, 2010; Subramanian, 2013). Realists believe what we see, and touch is a mere image of the true phenomena beyond our perception. Put differently, an excellent understanding of phenomena, especially in project management, is still improbable, if not illusory; conceptualizations and flawed methodologies sway the way we perceive realities.

Moreover, while qualitative research is mired in subjectivity, the quantitative method is objective but narrow. Therefore, it cannot explicate diverse idiosyncratic, behavioral, ethnocentric, and environmental dimensions of project management phenomena. Unlike realists, idealists believe that the only thing that is real is our perception of reality and that phenomena do not have to be broken into parts to understand them as the reductionists do; they think truth knowledge is acquired from a holistic view (Bergman et al., 2013; Ryan, 2015; Thielke, 2013; Turpin, 2015). In summary, the disparity in how we understand reality can impair theory translation to practical application.

The Quandary of PM/IT Methodologies

Organizations perceive software development methods as the antidotes to obsolescent, sluggish, and unsystematized information systems (Yakovleva, 2014). To access data faster, provide unparalleled customer service, develop, and market a product or service more quickly than their competitors, organizational leaders have invested trillions of dollars annually in the software development industry worldwide (Serrador and Pinto, 2015; Valle and O'Mara, 2015). The outcomes of these investments, however, have been a disappointment to many. To maximize shareholders' capital, a plethora of software development methodologies have emerged over the decades. The salient include the Systems Development Lifecycle (SDLC), also known as the Waterfall, Agile, and Prince2. Agile belongs to a family of software developing methodologies. It consists of SCRUM, Extreme Programming (XP), Spiral, Crystal, and Dynamic System Development Method, to name a few (Conforto et al., 2014). Matos and Lopes (2013) and Valle and O'Mara (2015) indicated that a project's methodology is essential in task measurement and control.

They explained that the PMBOK was created to guide PM practitioners to achieve PM tasks successfully. Creswell (2003) considered methodology as a strategic plan linked to results.

Generally, these methodologies differ on managing a project's scope, how to deliver the results, and how to engage stakeholders in the process. While the Waterfall methodology focuses on preplanning the scope and providing the work packages sequentially, the Agile family of methods employs an adaptive and iterative approach to software development. They neither preplan the scope nor deliver or release the work package or sprint sequentially. The project's scope is progressively elaborated and produced or released incrementally. They also require proactive and high-level stakeholders' engagement in the process. A coterie of team members works in a closely proximate milieu where each communicates directly facing the others.

Projects in Control Environments (Prince2) are practiced mainly in Great Britain and most European states (Matos and Lopes, 2013). Prince2 provides a prescriptive and normative approach to project management. Its raison d'etre is coterminous to business enterprises' undertakings. It guides practitioners to identify a business objective and mobilize resources to achieve that objective. Prince2 method requires high-level project team visibility. The project manager serves as the person responsible for the project. Like PM methodology, Prince2 initiates, plans, executes, controls, and closes projects (Matos and Lopes, 2013).

Despite their disparate approaches to managing project scope and delivering a product or service, these software development methodologies are commonly constrained by time, cost, scope, and quality. Studies show that their approaches are integrated into other industries (Conforto et al., 2014; Matos and Lopes, 2013). Serrador and Pinto (2015) indicated that, compared to the Waterfall method, Agile is a better methodology in the software development industry; it is adaptive and flexible. Its practitioners respond to risks more promptly and expeditiously. Puri (2009), however, noted that while Agile focuses on knowledge-self-managed workers, its process does not work well in a large crowd and complex environment.

Moreover, while PM's focus has been the software delivery cycle, how well stakeholders are engaged in the process, and how the project teams are supposed to meet, they have disregarded the PM. IT software development project's ontological perspective market has become due to PPGE. Yadav (2016) acknowledged that globalization had shifted software development from a co-located model (onsite) to an offshore model that involves the collaboration of a network of distributed teams and developers from across national frontiers.

PM practitioners should first understand the project's environment, ontology, epistemology, axiology, contextualization, and conceptualization before deciding what method to use or choose. The ontological perspective of PPGE asks the questions: what is PPGE? What does it constitute? Is it linear, nonlinear, complex, uncertain, and undefinable? The epistemological perspective will ask: What set of knowledge acquisitions do we need to unravel PPGE's weakness and benefit? In other words, what skill set is required to fully understand and meet PPGE-based organizational and, often, incompatible stakeholders' expectations? How do we know the behavior, volatility, interaction, success, and failure of projectification, programmification, and globalization? The axiological perspective poses the question: Do literature review, our internal analysis, and personal view help us ascertain untainted and unbiased understanding about PM phenomena? (Creswell, 2003, 2014; Sullivan, 2009; Tallon, 2014; Venkatesh et al., 2013).

Moreover, questions concerning the methodology that practitioners may ask to include the following: How practical is it for an offshore or virtual team to meet face-to-face? How do co-located team members achieve project goals in a PPGE-based, complex, chaotic, and nonlinear? Indeed, knowledge of PMBOK and applying a software development methodology alone is insufficient to riposte the multifaced risks (the unknowns and unknowns) that globalization continually presents.

PMT 2.0 intends to bridge the ontological gap between applying these methodologies and PM phenomena. PMT 2.0 espouses the notion that knowledge is the game changer between project mortality (chaos) and immortality (sustainability) and that continuous acquisition of knowledge about phenomena is propitious to a project's success (sustainability). In other words, if an advanced understanding of PM complexity, nonlinearity, and uncertainty is essential to PM, then the relationship between phenomena and the achievement of business or project objectives can be positive, negative, or none.

PM Methodology Selection Intelligence (PMMSI)

What justifies the best project methodology selection is its capacity to solve a question comparably quickly by delivering the best and sustainable value. Research students, for example, know what they must go through to convince their research team, advisors, or professors of their choice of research study methodology. However, the research methodology selection will not consistently optimize stakeholders' value if it remains incompatible with the research's purpose. Moreover, just as the surgeons must perform a preoperative diagnosis before surgeries, project management practitioners must understand PPG organisms and species well enough before selecting the project method. PMMI process includes the form and structure, concept, and context of PPG object phenomena. It also consists of a learning method or research methodology that practitioners can apply to entirely understand each part of the projects operating within the PPG context. The next is to select the appropriate approach that will deliver and achieve the components individually and collectively. The fourth process focuses on the project value that the method's application will optimize or maximize. The last phase is how putting together all PMMI elements will be communicated to the project stakeholders. In other words, PMMS Intelligence thinkers must focus on understanding the PPGE effect on the PM landscape, design, or develop a method conducive and propitious to their projects. PPGE realm is complex, arduous, and requires forethought and a deep understanding of the interconnectivity and dynamism among stakeholders across borders.

PM practitioners must ask themselves the following questions:

- First, what is PPGE, its impacts, and what does it constitute?
- Second, how do we learn about the concept, context, and extent of PPGE phenomena? Do I have adequate knowledge about PPGE? What kind of world am I investigating? What are the nature and the structure of PPGE realities? Often, the way we learn about facts determines success or failure. The profound and relevant our knowledge, the better our expertise of PPGE phenomena. On the other hand, the superficial, shallow, and irrelevant understanding of PPGE concepts, the fragile or myopic our decision and knowledge, and therefore the more quickly our project become susceptible to failure. It takes a doctor more than a decade to learn and to perfect his career. That is why the number of patients that die due to medical faults, errors, and leadership is negligible compared to the number of projects that fail. While the two are incomparable, a profound understanding of reality can differentiate between success and failure. Imagine a world where about 60 percent of patients die every year from a doctor or medical malefaction. Also imagine, how much a 60 percent megaproject failure costs stakeholders or taxpayers across the world. Moreover, imagine the sunk costs that incur due to the cancellation and abandonment of projects such as the Keystone Gas or Canadian Pipeline and projects of that ilk that are do not make the headline or included in the total project mortality costs.

The strategies of inquiry into PPGE nature do not always have to be the more straightforward method to run. The so-called popular quantitative has waned, especially in the social and human sciences, so much endemic and required to grasp the intricacies of operating in a PPGE environment fully. Fortunately, what has come of age is the hybrid of qualitative and quantitative methods. If applied well and all protocols adhered to, the hybrid method does a better job juxtaposing filters and unfiltered pieces of information needed to know the realities of PPGE constructs or complex situations.

- Third, what method can we apply that is the most simple, appropriate, effective, and efficient? Does the methodological choice I have made help achieve the desired outcomes? Project methods can be Waterfall, SCRUM, Agile, and Prince2, to name few examples.

- Fourth, does the identification of PPGE makeup, the knowledge that I have acquired about the PPGE impact, and the methodology I selected will help sustain client value? The focus must be normalizing values intrinsic to communities, societies. Obtaining maximum values is also about asking whether the project execution considers and respects cultural ethnic-religious values?

- Fifth, and how can I use emotional intelligence to communicate with all the project stakeholders even in the face of conflict or resistance? PM practitioners must demonstrate mature consciousness and emotionality and take actions that maximize the chance of successfully achieving project goals. In other words, the PMMS Intelligence is adaptable. It flourishes well in a continuous learning environment and can acquire and apply knowledge and skills. Adaption means that they must be willing to learn from experience, solve problems, and adapt to new situations.

The Paradox of Integrating Temporality and Permanence

Although organizational management operations and project management functions are multidisciplinary and thrive to maximize capital return, they are separate in their nature, function, and perception (Kuura et al., 2013; Malbasic et al., 2014). Organizational management teams and PM practitioners achieve their overarching objective through mobilizing resources, planning, organizing, controlling, and coordinating multiple tasks and activities. While PM is established to function temporally (Gransberg et al., 2013; Project Management Institute [PMBOK Guide], 2013), PPGE-based organizations are structured to operate semi-permanently or permanently. Ylijoki (2016) indicated that a project is inherently time-dependent: it is temporal, completes tasks within a fixed period, begins and ends, and does not promise or commit to function in perpetuity.

The integration of PM temporaneous function and the perpetual operation of PPGE-based organizations has raised significant conceptual, contextual, and theoretical challenges to PM as a distinct academic discipline field, including PM practitioners, but seems downright paradoxical. How does the trilogy's current concept, for instance, effectively perform in manifold complex, uncertain and nonlinear structures in which PPGE operates? How will PM practitioners handle macro, horizontal and vertical levels in PPGE-based organizational hierarchy? Jalocha (2012) noted that due to projectification expansion drives, the European Union had created thousands of mega-projects throughout member countries. An attempt to harmonize public and private programs is becoming a reality. Godenhjelm et al. (2014) explained that PM temporal existence and innovative capacity might be overshadowed or fragmented by the complex and monolithic structure that PPGE creates. In other words, the conflation of permanent and temporal functions presents a paradigm shift and a significant organizational and cultural change.

To better explain, describe and predict the success and failure of PPGE-based organizational objectives in a sustainable way, the PM domain must absorb the knowledge about these new conceptualizations, cultural, and organizational changes. Miles (2012) noted that organizations that absorb new knowledge are prone to become innovative, competitive, and successful.

PMT 2.0 is being developed to resolve the epistemological gap between the current PM theory and the PM domain because of the PPGE efforts (Wilkinson et al., 2015). Andersen (2015) and Bredillect (2008) classified project management practitioners into two perspectives: task management team and organization management team. They explained that while the former team focuses on the temporal nature of phenomena, i.e., to create a unique product or service and deliver it on time, on budget, and without diminishing its quality, the latter is focused on achieving short, as well as long-term, strategic goals. Scranton (2014) indicated that PM is distinguishable from organizational management because of time constraints, the urgency of project completion, a focus on a target, temporal project team, and achieving predetermined change.

The PMBOK Guide also pins down practitioners to observe the processes of a project's life cycle composed of initiation, planning, implementation, and closure, including PMBOK knowledge areas (Brunson, 2013). These areas consist of project integration, scope, cost, time, quality, human resource, communication, risk, procurement, and stakeholders' management (Project Management Institute [PMBOK Guide], 2013).

In PM's perspective, tasks are prescribed and planned at the project's onset and followed through completion. The stocks in trade practitioners apply to achieve this perspective are work breakdown structure (WBS), critical path method (CPM), precedence diagraming method (PDM), project evaluation review technique (PERT), network planning, and risk analysis, to name few examples. Suppose a change management problem arises, such as added work or risk. In that case, the preplanning phase process is reiterated, time is extended, additional resources are added, and the communication plan is updated. The project's stakeholders or owners may also decide to terminate the project prematurely if the total costs, including administrative, risk, net present value, and sunk costs, are higher than the project's potential benefit (PMBOK Guide, 2013). This perspective is also bereft of or detached from the rest of the community, society, or the world (Brunson, 2013).

Regarding organization perspective, practitioners pursue business opportunities, contribute to productivities, organizational success, or value creation on a steady or permanent continuum and seriatim. This involves planning, organizing, controlling, and coordinating. Pugh and Hickson (2007) noted that organizations might also be interested in pursuing endless activities such as manufacturing, commercial, marketing, security, accounting, and managerial endeavors. Thus, practitioners, many of whom are hired permanently rather than temporarily, set strategic and long-term goals rather than a short time and temporal objectives (Brunson, 2013). Moreover, rather than focusing on controlling cost, quality, and earned value analysis as task management practitioners do, the organizational perspective tends to embrace a holistic view on business or organization value creation.

Greenwood and Miller (2010) also indicated that PM and organizational functions' duration or longevity were not paralleled. PM's choice of design is based on its innovativeness, efficiency, and cost-effectiveness. It is based on normative and prescriptive standards and tools used to complete a project's deliverables quickly. Collectively, project and organizational stakeholders perceive PM as an antidote to bureaucracies, inefficient management, and prolongation of management functions (Kwak et al., 2015). The pursuit of this lofty ideal compels PM practitioners to work on a tight budget, time, quality, and scope that is unambiguously defined and executed.

Organizational functions are not constrained by temporality, bureaucratic structure, and the triple constraint conceptualizations (Garel, 2012). PM methods and approaches, especially the trilogy concept, cannot address complex issues beyond the scope (technical), cost (budget), quality, and time (schedule). Consequently, irrespective of astronomical investment in managing projects, the rate of project successes continues to shrink. Kwak et al. (2015) argued that projects become the units of control and PM in project-based organizational milieus, the governance of the relationships between the units, and other activities inside and outside the organizational settings.

Comparison between PM Theory and PMT 2.0

The research study will gather raw data from multiple sources, including unfiltered open-ended interviews, archival documents, direct observations, policy papers, survey data, and annual reports to compare PM theory and PM theory 2.0. As opposed to a closed-ended question based on short answers, an open-ended question questionnaire encourages participants to express, fully, their views, real feelings, attitudes, or experiences about PM phenomena. This can lead to an unexpected discovery from participant responses. An open-ended questionnaire also encourages participants to adequately address complex, chaotic, uncertain, and nonlinear PM phenomena. The study used the researched pieces of information to compare data from one case unit of analysis to another, industry to industry, PM chapter member participants to another PM chapter member participants, and PM practitioners from one site to another (Sbaraini et al., 2011; Yin, 2014). In other words, the study used data to perform cross-case synthesis, literal replication, and pattern matching (Yin, 2014).

The results were evaluated on seven theoretical propositions, participant responses to the research questions, literature reviews, and the four basic theoretical elements' criteria. The essential elements include definition, domain, relationships, and predictive capacity. Furthermore, the results were tested based on the eight criteria of virtues of a good theory. These virtues of a good theory are uniqueness, parsimony, conservation, generalizability, fecundity, internal consistency, empirical riskiness, and abstraction (Gelso, 2006; Harlow, 2009, 2010; Wacker, 1998) (see Figure 1).

The research goal was to provide an in-depth understanding of these theories, examine whether they were aligned with or relevant to PM phenomena due to PPGE efforts, had internally consistent relationships among the constructs, and met the criteria of virtues of a good theory (Greenwald, 2012; Naor et al., 2013). A choice of good and virtuous theory is essential to the realm of project management. Unfortunately, PM practitioners and training institutions rarely weigh the potential benefits and risks of a PM theory before practice. Connelly (2014) showed that the absence of theory could misguide practitioners.

The Project Management Institute's Project Management Body of Knowledge (PMIBOK) Guide derived from various grand scale theories and canonical practices such as Eliyahu M. Goldratt's seminal theory of constraints, the work breakdown structure, earned value management, critical path method, and program evaluation procedure technique and projects portfolio management (Padalkar and Gopinath, 2015; Simsit et al., 2014). Due to PPGE efforts, the project management field has shifted gears from a mere emphasis on a project's scope, time, and cost to apply a holistic approach to managing projects. The manifold interconnected and interdependent constraints that the project management domain constitutes, along with the dismal failures of projects across industries to complete projects on time and within budget, has sparked intensive theoretical debate among project management practitioners.

Two theory development process areas are deductive (deterministic) and inductive (interpretative) (Bland and Roberts-Pittman, 2014). The deductive and deterministic cause and effect approach to theory building answers the how and why questions. These questions and answers explain the fundamental justification of the theory and the interrelationships among the constructs. The interpretative and inductive approach focuses on the who, where, how, and what questions about theory development instead of believing that knowledge is absolute (Taephant et al., 2015). Wacker (1998) also included the should, could, and would questions. The "what" identifies and describes phenomena and arranges constructs or variables in a logical order. The where defines the theory's boundary and answers questions about abstraction and generalizability parameters (Byron and Thatcher, 2016; Crane et al., 2016). Studies show that understanding and genuinely predicting phenomena in the project management domain, including its manifold and uncertain constructs, requires the combined application of deductive and inductive approaches (Yoshikawa et al., 2013).

Understanding the impact of PPGE makes the application of PMT2.0 theory conducive and comparable to the project management field and managing megaprojects. PMT2.0 describes, explains, and predicts events as nonlinear, adaptive, self-organizing, holistic, and unpredictable (Bergman et al., 2013; Maranon and Pera, 2015). The concern that has remained unanswered is that, despite its expansion due to PPGEs that function beyond the classic trilogy and lifecycle, project management theory has remained stagnated and disconnected from these new realities. PM theory 2.0 (PMT2.0) is proposed as an alternative to the PM extant theory. PMT2.0 views phenomena in terms of three conceptualizations: sustainable competitive edge (immortality), chaos (mortality), and advanced knowledge (the game changer). The manifold and interconnected issues that project management practitioners encounter in managing projects, especially PPGE-based projects, cannot be resolved through prescriptive solutions. The survival of project management, as we know it, depends on how dissimilar, interconnected stakeholders, legal, economic, cultural, linguistic, and environmental boundaries will interact and self-organize to share information and create innovative, efficient, and effective, and practical solutions to managing projects. The sustainability (immortality) and competitiveness of a project depend on the harmony, unflinching commitment, and cooperation that the web of individuals and institutions will establish. Contrarily, suppose the stakeholders and PM practitioners do not create a fertile, collaborative, and harmonious working environment? In that case, the chance to deliver a project on time will doom, fail or die.

In an ethnographic field study of the Panama Canal expansion megaproject, for instance, Marewijk and Smits (2015) found that the cultural attributes such as governing style and lifeways influenced the way employees made crucial project decisions. Ignorance of the dynamic of culture and how it impacts the way employees make decisions in a particular environment can stymie progress and is, therefore, chaotic. Advanced knowledge or continuous learning (the game changer) will focus on technical savoir-faire and encompass a profound understanding of intercultural communication, projectification, programmification, and globalization. It will determine and predict the survivability of the project; it can alter the status of a portended and imminently chaotic situation. PMT 2.0 will describe, explain, and predict PM's complex nature due to PPGE efforts.

The Theory of PM Theory 2.0

PMT 2.0 defines a project as temporary, semipermanent, or permanent undertakings created to develop a specific product or provide a service to achieve a specific goal or objectives. PMT 2.0 defines 2.0 postulates that word temporary cannotes few months or a year, but it will not mean over ten years except in hyperbole or when speaking figuratively. It took over ten years to finish the Panama Canal, a decade to complete the Three Gorges Dam of China, over four years to build the Golden Gate Bridge, generations to construct the Great Pyramid of Giza, and over twenty years to build the Great Wall of China.

Figure XY

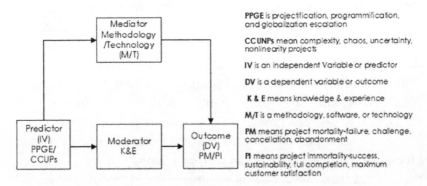

PMT 2.0 spurs knowledge and enlightenment and undergirds project management practitioners and business leaders to boost their capacity to manage and complete PPGE-based projects. It also explains the extent of PPGE concepts in enlarging the PM domain, describes the interaction among PPGE constructs, predicts PM phenomena, and proposes the application of PPGE variables to intervene and solve real project management problems by following its quartet formulation:

- As figure XY shows, PPGE-CCUPs predict a positive or negative correlation with project failure or success (i.e., with every other variable remaining constant, the execution of complex projects may lead to project mortality or immortality).
- The moderator, KE, affects the strength and direction between PPGE-CCUPs and project mortality or

immortality. The more educated, skilled, and experienced the megaproject management team, the better the positive relationship between PPGE and the outcome. The higher the knowledge and experience, the better the chance of reducing the project mortality rate.

- Methodology or technology is the game changer. The wrong project method or software can lead to project mortality. iIf the PM practitioners do not choose the project method wisely, it will hurt the project.

PPGE is the predictor, PM or I, the outcome, and CCUNP, the mediator. Knowledge is the moderator. The predictor (independent variable) affects the outcome (Dependent Variable). The mediator explains the extent to which the predictor (PPGE) influences, causes, or controls the outcome (mortality). CUUNP is related to or associated with PPGE and mortality. The moderator or the intervention mechanism influences the magnitude of the predictor's effect on the outcomes (DV).

Simply put, PPGE's expansion directly impacts project mortality or immortality and directly elevates the CCUNP level of complexity. The extent to which PPGE has affected project failure seemed to replicate across construction, transportation, information technology, health care, pharmaceutics, management, and education industries. Knowledge and experience are the moderators, the game-changing mechanism. The less the knowledge and experience managing complex projects increase the risks and reduce project completion rate.

In other words, a complex project is riskier, is more likely to fail, overruns cost, more challenging, takes years or decades to complete. Overwhelmingly, the research study participants supported Proposition 3, which asserts that a complete knowledge of PPGE constructs changes PM mortality to immortality. In other words, most respondents agreed that knowledge of PPGE constructs was the game changer.

PPGE has expanded PM extant theory domain beyond the iron triangle viz. scope, cost, and schedule (Artto et al., 2015; Godenhjelm et al., 2014; Rijke et al., 2014). The expansion has also gone beyond the temporality and project lifecycle contextualization. This limited vista makes PM extant theory ineffective in predicting events that may drive organizations to succeed or fail. Garel (2012) indicated PM has no theory but orchestrated and tested prescriptive practices, standards, and tools. Studies show that managing project uncertainty and predictability is crucial to achieving sustainable success (Parker et al., 2015). For instance, a pharmaceutical firm and program-based may find it conducive and propitious to use its internal and standard operating procedure rather than follow a PM prescriptive and pre-determined template or process. Another essential drawback of PM current theory is the absence of interconnected relationships between its constructs considering the PPGE effects (Wilkinson et al., 2015). This makes it more challenging, if not impossible, to predict the relationship between PM extant theory and constructs of complex projects.

The reality is that the effects of PPGE have expanded the PM base integrating the PM Body of Knowledge processes and the core function of program manager's strategic responsibilities, including improving performance, fostering sustainable growth, and maximizing ROI and competitiveness (Huarng and Mas-Tur, 2016). The integration of project and program, for instance, constitutes a challenge to PM's notion of the temporality and finite nature of projects; program-oriented projects operate semi-permanently or permanently.

One of the viable components of programmification is resource management accomplished via project portfolio management application (PPM) to manage resource scarcity. In the absence of relationships between constructs, it becomes impossible to predict projects both in the short and long terms (Parker et al., 2015). Rigby et al. (2014) indicated that PM's problem is not whether a theory is absent. The problem is the missing of a coherent description, explanation, and prediction of phenomena. PMT2.0 explicitly defines and describes the PM domain's limits and creates relationships between and among the constructs. It comprises the capacity to predict events about complex, uncertain, and chaotic phenomena.

PMT2.0 provides the answers to the who, what, when, where, how, why, should, and would question. It addresses the complexity and the enlargement of PM current theory that the escalation of pro-jectification, programmification, and globalization has created. The theory's goodness and virtue fit will be analyzed and explained using the PM domain as a case in point (Artto et al., 2015; Godenhjelm et al., 2014; Rijke et al., 2014). PMT2.0 was evaluated against the criteria and virtues of good theory (see Appendix L). These virtues and the good of theory are as follows: uniqueness, parsimony, con-servatism, generalizability, fecundity, internal consistency, empirical riskiness, and abstraction (Wacker, 1998, p. 364). These evaluation processes also contribute to either verifying an old assumption or testing a new one about phenomena, thus contributing to a theory's building.

The project management field is being expanded rapidly due to successes in projectification, programmification, and globalization efforts. Any research that intends to contribute in a meaningful or significant way to theory in this domain must consider the linear (deterministic and inductive) and nonlinear (holistic and deduc-tive) dimensions that result from these expansions. If deductive, the researcher may start with a hypothesis intended to test cause and effect relationships between variables such as traditional and mod-ern project management methodologies. In the inductive case, the researcher begins with an observation and questions and builds the data theory (Ellis and Levy, 2008).

Harlow (2009) and Stam (1998, 2000, 2006, 2010) indicated a symbiotic relationship between research data and theory and that expanding our understanding of data leads to a theory. Understanding PM's complex nature helps the researcher cogently define and explain the phenomena and accurately predict events based on conceptual foundations.

The research contributes to theory through methods specific to three categories as follows: (a) analytical, conceptual research, (b) case study, and (c) empirical statistical research. The application of case studies is propitious to build theory (Wacker, 1998). Stam (1996, 2000, 2006, 2010) and Harlow (2009) acknowledged the significance of case studies in contributing to theory development. They explained that a case study could disprove the viability of an existing theory and, therefore, can potentially contribute to theory building through empirical evidence and testing. Studies show that theory development and testing are interconnected (Harlow, 2010).

Through retroduction, a researcher can retest a theory when a new set of data is discovered that can determine whether the new discovery is significant enough to replace the existing theory. A theory can be developed by interpreting new realities or facts gathered through interviews, surveys, literature reviews, and archival documents. Harlow (2009, 2010) stated that the process of theory development is recursive or cyclical: the researcher can gather data through observations, surveys, interviews, or case studies to test an extant theory. If the data fail to validate the theory, the researcher can reject the research or place a moratorium on it and start an entirely new project. However, if the data provide sufficient empirical evidence to invalidate the current theory, a new theory is espoused.

The analytical, conceptual research method encourages creativity, innovation, and organization of concepts or constructs. It creates internally consistent logical relationships among complex and abstract concepts. Like an empirical case study, this method gathers data through a case study as evidence to validate what the researcher assumes about these conceptualizations. The researcher can draw information or ideas from experience, conceptual modeling, and hermeneutics, i.e., interpretation or deduction of facts from observation to develop theory. Empirical, experimental design examines and tests performances, differences among the old and new theory, including the cause-and-effect relationships among variables or constructs, some of which can be direct or indirect, endogenous or exogenous (Solaiman et al., 2016). The study investigators examined and tested various hypothetical scenarios by putting some control mechanism during the research, including whether projectification, programmification, and globalization efforts have created a significant mismatch between current project management theory and the complex and nonlinear realities of the project management domain.

Defining PMT 2.0 (what and who).

PMT2.0 defines a project as temporary or permanent undertakings created to develop a product or provide a service to achieve a specific objective. PMT2.0 is based on a tripartite concept. The first part (project) is characterized by complexity, chaos, uncertainty, and nonlinearity (mortality). This is the result of PPGE expansion efforts. The second part (knowledge) is a game changer and power broker. Immortality (sustainability, competitive edge, maximization of ROI that endures) is the third part. The three-step tripartite process is comprehensively explained in a five-step process (see Appendix M). The knowledge objective can be PPGE-based micro-training, PPGE-based macro training, continuous learning, and hiring or retaining knowledge practitioners. Study proposition 4 stated that if knowledge is the game changer between project mortality and immortality, then the continuous acquisition of knowledge about phenomena is propitious to a project's success. In other words, if the advanced knowledge of PM complexity, nonlinearity, and uncertainty is essential to PM, then the relationship between phenomena and the achievement of business or project objectives can be positive, negative, or none.

According to PMT 2.0, project professionals must thoughtfully acquire some level of knowledge and experience about the manifold challenges and chaos of PM phenomena to achieve the what and who. Lundy and Morin (2013) and Reich et al. (2013) indicated deeper knowledge and an effective application of knowledge about phenomena determine the power and strength to effect positive change within project, program, and globally oriented organizations. It also helps reduce the failure (mortality) rate of complex projects.

The depth of knowledge about phenomena will further enable practitioners to become knowledgeable employees able to self-organize, self-manage, self-sustain, interconnect, and collaborate. A progressive, effective, and efficient collaboration will produce a better-negotiated contract, attract funding agencies, shareholders, and put in place creative and innovative policies that will sustain short and long-term business objectives. Kuura et al. (2013) argued that the development of a highly skilled and competent workforce had led many countries, including United States, China, UK, and Australia, to improve performance and, consequently, bolster and increase PM success rate.

The definition of "who" or "what" constructs refer to how projectification, programmification, and globalization efforts have expanded PM's theoretical domain. Besides the complex, uncertain and unpredictable nature of PM phenomena, the domain of PMT 2.0 includes resource scarcity, shortage of macro-trained professionals or knowledge employees, the rarity of complexity in procurements, equipment, and increased difficulty in obtaining physical capital (Brahm and Tarzan, 2015). Other chaos elements comprise market constraints, currency fluctuations, unstable political and economic systems, disparate management styles, legal, social, psychological, cultural, and environmental factors. PMT 2.0 espouses the notion that weak and nebulous definition of phenomena can undermine the theoretical underpinnings practitioners need to squarely and unmistakably focus attention on the fundamental PM management challenges that PPGE creates (Gelso, 2006; Harlow, 2009; Wacker, 1998).

Limiting the domain (when and where)

PM extant theory's domain is constricted to PPGE; it fails to address when the unpredictable will occur and where the complex realities exist. In other words, the PM theory is limited to temporality and projects' lifecycle contextualization. PM theory argues that a project's objective of completing deliverables is only achieved by sequentially following specific predetermined phrases and prescriptive formats or templates. These formats include completing the project according to scope, time (schedule), cost (budget), and quality management. The phrases are initiation, planning, execution or implementation, monitoring and control, and project termination. The limited vista of PM theory regarding PPGE makes its predictability inutile (Parker, Parsons, and Isharyanto, 2015).

Moreover, while mega or transnational projects limit PM current theory to completely describe, explain, and make predictions about these various PM phenomena, PMT 2.0 domain is capable of comprehensively explaining PPGE-based organizational activities. A theory domain is a place and location that events occur in the project's lifecycle or organization.

The PMT 2.0 postulates that knowledge is a game changer between a chaotic situation and business success. An accurate understanding of complex and nonlinear phenomena reduces the risk of misalignment and mismatch between theory and practice. It also increases the power of PPGE events' predictability (Hartman et al., 2013; Thamhain, 2013).

Relationship building (why and how). The effects of PPGE increase project and business complexity (chaos) or mortality rate. It also heightens tension, conflict, risk and makes tradeoffs more challenging and, sometimes, impossible (Thamhain, 2013). Micro, meso, macro training and learning and knowledge employees can alter and transform a chaotic situation (weakness) into a strength. This is achievable through the efforts of knowledge practitioners who are self-organized, collaborative, and self-sustained.

PMT 2.0 guides practitioners to understand PPGE semantics through four fundamental conceptualizations explained in a five-step process (see appendix M). The elements of this quartet conceptualization are:

- The independent variable, PPGE-CCUPs, predicts a positive or negative correlation with project failure or success (i.e., with every other variable remaining constant, the execution of complex projects may lead to project mortality or immortality).
- The moderator, knowledge, and experience (KE) affect the strength and direction between PPGE-CCUPs and project mortality or immortality (DV).
- The more educated, skilled, and experienced the megaproject management team, the better the positive relationship between PPGE and the outcome. The higher the knowl-

edge and experience, the better the chance of reducing the project mortality rate.

- The mediator, method, or technology (M/T) is an interventionist agent or the game changer. The more fitting the method, software, hardware, strategy, and tactics to the scope and environment of the project, the more on target, on budget, and satisfying the outcome.

PPGE is the predictor, PM or I, the outcome, and CCUNP, the mediator. Knowledge is the moderator. The predictor (independent variable) affects the outcome (Dependent Variable). The mediator explains the extent to which the predictor (PPGE) influences, causes, or controls the outcome (mortality). CUUNP is related to or associated with PPGE and mortality. The moderator or the intervention mechanism influences the magnitude of the predictor's effect on the outcomes (DV).

Simply put, PPGE's expansion directly impacts project mortality or immortality and indirectly elevates the CCUNP level of complexity. The extent to which PPGE has affected project failure seemed to replicate across construction, transportation, information technology, health care, pharmaceutics, management, and education industries. Knowledge and experience are the moderators, the game-changing mechanism. The less the knowledge and experience managing complex projects increase the risks and reduce project completion rate.

This study believes that an essential part of the performance stagnation and doldrums in PM is the absence of 21st-century organic governance and efficient knowledge of and application of technology. The wise and efficient knowledge practitioners can create novel working approaches, unleash innovation and creativity, and turn chaotic, complex, and unpredictable phenomena into unimagined success (Gelso, 2006; Harlow, 2009, 2010; Wacker, 1998).

PMT 2.0 predictive assumptions (could, should, and would).

Drawing from the seminal human capital theory, PMT 2.0 postulates a correlation between educational advancement and business or project success (Bae and Patterson, 2014; Kaba, 2013). PMT 2.0's prediction of phenomena is based on the following eight propositions: Proposition 1: If a good and virtuous theory provides a full description, definition, explanation, and prediction of phenomena, PM's theoretical boundary will expand due to PPGE efforts. Proposition 2: If full description, definition, and prognosis of PM phenomena undergird PM practitioners, then a complete understanding of phenomena due to PPGE is propitious to PM success. Proposition 3: If project practitioners have little or no theoretical underpinnings about complex phenomena, then translating theory into practice will become impractical or negative. This exposes innocuous undertakings to a plethora of risks and can lead to a project mortality. Proposition 4: If knowledge is the game changer between project mortality and immortality, then the continuous acquisition of knowledge about phenomena is propitious to a project's success. In other words, if the advanced knowledge of PM complexity, nonlinearity, and uncertainty is essential to PM, then the relationship between phenomena and the achievement of business or project objectives can be positive, negative, or none. Proposition 5: If a theory meets the criteria of a good and a virtuous theory, as measured by the criteria drawing from Gelso (2006), Harlow (2009, 2010), and Wacker (1998), then a complete understanding of phenomena due to PPGE efforts will increase and, as a result, translating theory into practice will be more accurate and predictable. Proposition 6: If the new constructs or neologisms such as PPGE expand PM territorial boundaries, the extant theory must expand to accommodate the neologisms. Otherwise, a superior theory should be developed to understand better the new PM phenomena (Coff and Raffile, 2015). Proposition 7: If knowledge workers are the sources of sustainable competition, then effective, efficient, and progressive knowledge practitioners can offset the relationship between complexity, uncertainty, chaos, and a project's success or immortality (Coff and Raffile, 2015).

In other words, PMT2.0 predicts the occurrence of one or all of the following scenarios: (There is a relationship between the management of complex and chaotic projects and the achievement of business or project objectives. This relationship can be positive, negative, and none. A macro knowledge of complex phenomena reduces or eliminates the vicissitudes of complex and chaotic projects, programs, and globally interconnected business operations. Knowledge practitioners change the relationship between complexity and success. Effective, efficient, and progressive collaboration among stakeholders can promote dialogue sharing of information. This can enable practitioners to resolve issues, create harmony among complex units, and create innovative and sustainable or win-win solutions to complex projects and chaotic situations. The less the knowledge of complicated and messy project tasks, the more perilous and elusive the answers will become. In other words, when project practitioners have little or no theoretical underpinnings about complex phenomena, the translation of theory into practice becomes impractical and negative. This exposes innocuous undertakings to a plethora of risks and can lead to project failure.

Criteria of Virtues of Good Theory

PMT 2.0 is unique; it is different from theories of operation management science. The combination of variables or constructs and conceptualizations is also uniquely disparate. A project's mortality and chaotic elements constitute various and nonlinear characteristics descriptive of what the PM field has become due to the PPGE (Nasir et al., 2015). The following elements determine a good and theory's virtues:

Conservatism

As a linear, methodological, and philosophical neutral, PMT 2.0 provides a more precise definition and description of PPGE constructs. It can predict events based on its internal constructs and the extent of their interconnectedness, correlation, and symbiotic relationships. PPGE's expansion, for instance, directly impacts mortality and indirectly elevates the CCUNP level of complexity. The more PPGE expands, the more complex, chaotic, uncertain, and nonlinear PM phenomena become, and the higher the challenge of achieving immortality.

Generalizability

Practitioners from across academic disciplines, industries, and borders can apply PMT2.0. It provides an in-depth explication of complex projects, especially PPGE-based organizations. The replication of complex, chaotic, uncertain, and nonlinear phenomena (CCUNP) across construction, transportation, information technology, health care, pharmaceutics, management, and education industries determine the strength of the association between CCUNP and PPGE (see Table 9).

Fecundity

As nonlinear and universally based, PMT 2.0 domain is not limited to temporaneous projects alone but the integration of temporary, semi-permanent, and permanent undertakings. It espouses the notion that since organizational activities have become boundaryless and timeless due to PPGE expansion efforts, PM theory must also expand to keep pace with the dynamic of organizational changes, including technological jolts and the effects of globalization. PMT2.0 defines and describes complex phenomena; it is scalable and customizable to any public and private organization across industries and borders irrespective of size.

Parsimony

PMT 2.0 provides a three-step approach to understanding how a complex organization's nature and dynamic expanded due to PPGE (Nasir et al., 2015). It also espouses fewer assumptions compared to the current PM theory.

Internal consistency

Internal consistency means the theory has identified and explained all relationships adequately among constructs or variables-independent and dependent (Gelso, 2006; Harlow, 2010; Wacker, 1998). The constructs or variables are relatable and interconnected. Some of the relationships among the constructs are correlated negatively and positively. A positive correlation means that the more the discovery of additional meanings of the project or phenomena, the better the understanding, description, and predictability. A negative correlation means regardless of what investment stakeholders make to offset certain trade-offs, the situation will remain negative. Zero correlation relationship means regardless of what practitioners may do; the situation will remain unaltered or constant.

These assumed or proposed relationships can be explained in the following formula: PPGE is the predictor of PM mortality. The higher the level of PPGE expansion, the more complex, chaotic, uncertain, and nonlinear PM phenomena become, and the less the chance of achieving immortality. Moreover, the higher the knowledge of these phenomena, the better the chance of converting mortality to immortality. The elements of this tripartite are mutually dependent as well as interdependent. A change in one also changes the dynamic of the others. The theory is not complex or dialectic; the key is to develop knowledge that will be of benefit and relevance to practitioners' comprehensive understanding of complex, nonlinear, and chaotic phenomena (Coff and Raffile, 2015; Godenhjelm et al., 2014; Rijke et al., 2014).

Drucker (1999) indicated that knowledge interweaves with management disciplines and therefore requires knowledge workers' productivity. They organize, collaborate, attend meetings, make calls, dialogue with many stakeholders, correct mistakes, evaluate models, and create an environment conducive to sustainability and high productivities. This requirement (the need for knowledge workers) is the game changer in twenty-first century PM, especially in the face of expanding the PM domain due to PPGE and the manifold and sometimes intractable challenges it poses. Kurt Goldstein (1934) taught that when employees are self-actualized, they can achieve self-fulfillment and holism, the individual's ability to better understand the complex environment and interconnect with it (Sparks and Repede, 2016; Whitehead, 2017). In exploring McGregor's X/Y theory, Lawter et al. (2015) indicated that, as opposed to those (the x group) who are micro-trained, lackadaisical, and lack motivations, most people (the group) are capable of self-direction and self-control and have the innate capacity to solve complex problems.

The knowledge worker concept is a direct antithesis to the non-knowledge or manual worker, unskilled or inexperienced worker. Knowledge workers seek to understand the tasks, execute, and complete them by eliminating the chaos, minimizing the uncertainties, and challenging the complexities. They begin with asking the right questions about tasks, environmental concerns, and their nature. Since PM sciences are dynamic and require new methodologies and techniques, they must adopt continuous learning, teaching, and innovation.

Furthermore, PMT2.0 describes and explicates phenomena as an interconnected web of constructs that interact nonlinearly. It espouses the notion that phenomena are unpredictable and adaptable. These characteristics will make PMT 2.0 internally consistent, predictable, and attractive by industrial experts and business organizations across many frontiers (Fenwick and Dahlgren, 2015).

In addition, PMT 2.0 philosophical foundation is based on the proposition that if PPGE efforts expand PM territorial boundaries, the extant theory must grow as well to accommodate these neologisms; otherwise, a superior theory should be developed to provide a better understanding of the nature of the new PM phenomena

(Coff and Raffile, 2015). These proposed foundations or constructs resonate with the structures of PPGE-based organizations. They will explain the relationship between projectification, programmification, and globalization constructs and describe ways to predict feasible events.

Empirical Riskiness

The theory is vulnerable and can be subjected to refutation if a given project's management team is unaware of its complexity. Another situation that may cause PMT 2.0 rebuttal is where its application may become uncommon or not required in achieving a business objective. A case in point is where only micro knowledge is needed to resolve complex and chaotic and uncertain projects.

Abstraction

PMT 2.0 is not delimited by time and space. It is open and can relate to additional neologisms or new constructs (Wacker, 1998).

PMT 2.0 Theoretical Foundation

The study drew most of the PMT 2.0 theoretical base from the instrumentalist perspective. The purpose of a virtuous and good theory is to undergird practitioners with full knowledge of phenomena, boost their performance or solve real problems (Greenwald, 2012; Huarng and Mas-Tur, 2016). This requires deep understanding, knowledge, expertise, and experience regarding PM phenomena' nature and environment. Swanson and Chermack (2013) indicated that theoretical application drives practitioners to identify a theory's weaknesses and strengths and seek further understanding.

Over decades, theoretical proponents, PM practitioners, and management scholars have striven to change the dismal project completion rate by identifying ills and paralyzes of project management and proposing new approaches to improve work performance and complete a project's deliverables based on baselines. Al-Ahmad et al. (2009) and Johnson et al. (2015) listed a glut of why projects fail. Some say project implementation failures are due to lack of adequate funding, competent project managers, stakeholders' engagement, leadership, and training, to mention few examples.

The Project Management Institute (PMI) proposed the Organizational Project Maturity Model (OPM3) to improve maturity in managing complex projects due to PPGE (Alami et al., 2015). Despite these efforts, the literature is riddled with evidence that shows the panaceas they proposed have not made any significant headway in the way PM practitioners implement projects (Neverauskas et al., 2013; Poston and Richardson (2010). Others claim that PMI and the plethora of rescue efforts and reforms are equally blamed for projects' implementation malaise; the extant PM theory still lacks a precise definition, description, and prediction about PM phenomena to PPGE efforts. Studies indicate that when a theory and practice are compatible, business firms produce positive impacts on the bottom line (Herbert et al., 2013). Kumar and Antonenko (2014) and Walker (2014) indicated that they coexist despite the difference between practice and theory.

PMT 2.0 is being developed because the PM current theory is incapable of defining, describe and predict the complexity, chaos, uncertainty, and nonlinearity of PM current realities. Besides its ability to recognize and provide a detailed definition, description, and prediction of what the PM domain has become due to PPGE, PMT2.0 is nuanced, scalable, and customizable (Lattimer, 2015; Vongprasuth and Choi, 2014). This provides an opportunity to project practitioners working on a project (big or small) first to understand the nature and environment of the project and therefore choose what is applicable, responsive, and effective to that specific context. Besides, PMT 2.0 theoretical underpinnings also provide a conceptual framework from which practitioners can work together to subdue, minimize, and eliminate the specters of project chaos, complexity, and uncertainty and to achieve sustainable success (Kumar and Antonenko, 2014).

Like other academic disciplines, project management's theoretical foundations expect PM practitioners to execute projects in a certain fashion. The enlargement of PM through PPGE, for instance, has increased the complexity and uncertainties of PM discipline (KapsaliBrowaldh, 2012; Vongprasuth and Choi, 2014). Thus, PM professionals are obligated to perform strategic and task-oriented operations and interconnect and collaborate with a plethora of components. They must also confront socioeconomic issues, technological, legal, cultural, linguistic impediments, and uncertainties spanning across multiple territorial jurisdictions.

To fully understand this complicated, interconnected web of complex realities, PM practitioners are required to link theory to practice (Thamhain, 2013). Walker (2014) asserted that the use of theory would cease if it remains isolated from practice. He indicated that irrespective of the dichotomous relationship between practice and theory, they coexist (Kumar and Antonenko, 2014).

Project Management Body of Knowledge (PMBOK) incorporates grand scale theory, minitheories, methodologies, and techniques to underpin PM practitioners to, among other things, have a better understanding of the theoretical foundation of project management and facilitate the translation of theory to practical application. In the construction industry, for instance, project practitioners are challenged to translate concepts into technical designs. Finding the appropriate and user-friendly technologies, including software that conforms to the construction's geometry, can be challenging. With the theoretical concepts in mind, when the project's execution phase veers off the blueprint or baseline, practitioners can easily detect the misalignment and take corrective actions. Educational institutions inculcate to their graduate programs exercises that can prepare students to connect theory and practice. In other words, the connection between practice and the relevant theories allows researchers and PM practitioners to refine their research goals and operationalize concepts in alignment with the theory that the research or organization attempts to translate into practice (Kumar and Antonenko, 2014).

The Application and Praxis of PM Theory

Feldman and Worline (2014) expressed skepticism about the repeated application of PM tools, methodologies, approaches, and standards on projects regardless of their idiosyncratic and environmental differences. They proposed, for practical application of theory and rationality, the exercise of subtleness and applying knowledge and tools appropriate to PM phenomena. They noted that a reasonable, rational application of theory enables practitioners to understand, engage, and improve the way PM theory is translated into reality. A project management team, for instance, may develop a different repertoire of essential tools that are relevant and appropriate to a local situation that its members can use to resolve their unique internal challenges. This helps organizations minimize the knowledge gap between applying prescriptive solutions and a diversified, dynamic, and complex PM environment but reap tremendous benefits from its members through self-sustaining, self-organizing, and information-sharing efforts.

Undoubtedly, PPGE expansion efforts have broadened the landscape, context, concept, and scope of project management discipline beyond the current theoretical foundation (Svejvig and Andersen, 2014; Ramazani and Jergeas, 2014). In 2010, PMI predicted that 15.7 million new positions would be created globally within a decade due to project management's economic footprint, including direct and indirect productive activities. PMP certification programs and certified PM managers have also increased by over 1,300 percent worldwide (Nasir et al., 2015). In other words, the domain of project management is entrenched and integrated into every aspect of academic disciplines, creating a litany of complex and interdisciplinary constructs, including programmification, portfolio management, project management maturity model, green projects, and sustainability, to name a few (Solaiman et al., 2016). While project management's context is expanding exponentially, the theory of project management remains stagnant and inertial.

This knowledge deficit places PM theory in a crisis and moribund state; practitioners' home-based knowledge is no longer adequate to fully understand the various PM challenges found in other countries (Herman and Handayani, 2015). Also, the acquisition of qualified experts, lack of resources, and lack of reliable infrastructure are challenges that PM practitioners must deeply understand and be prepared to confront to achieve sustainable overseas success.

This study attempts to develop a project management theory 2.0 (PMT2.0) to expand the scope of the extant theoretical underpinnings in line with current realities. The basis of PMT2.0 is self-organization, linear neutrality, eclecticism, and pragmatism. The self-organization/readjustment process enables stakeholders / social units from manifold backgrounds to mutually interact, learn and adapt, adjust or readjust to what emerges through their interaction. Linear neutralism acknowledges the notion that true knowledge of phenomena is not always predictable, linear, or deterministic; it is non-linear, unpredictable, and uncertain (Wilson et al., 2012). PMT2.0 is also fecund, unique, parsimonious, internally consistent, empirically risky, and abstractional (Zdanyte and Neverauskas, 2012). Del Marmol (2015) identified political, ecological, sociocultural, technological, legal, and economic factors to constitute PM complexity. He advocated that knowledge of these constructs is essential to PM success. Marewijk and Smits (2015) and Svejvig and Andersen (2014) indicated that local sensitivities such as the effects of ethnicity, tribal governance, and ceremonies are influential factors to consider when managing PPGE-based projects.

The success of research in academic disciplines, including project management, depends on theory. It is through research that a theory can be developed. Both theory and research are, therefore, interrelated. Through case studies, a researcher can gather efficient evidence that can disprove an extant theory and contribute to developing a theory. Miles (2012) and Wacker (1998) underscored the significant reciprocal rapport between theory and research. They suggested that a theory bolsters a researcher's ability to analyze and create well-organized methods for field development and is an explication and a prediction of phenomena. Studies show that a good theory can guide practitioners toward achieving the organization's mission and objective methodically in a well-organized and effective way (Miles, 2012; Swanson and Chermack, 2013). Levy and Ellis (2006) held a similar view that a theory provides the foundation as well as a description and explanation of the phenomena that the researcher investigates. Connelly (2014) showed that the absence of theory could misguide a researcher's efforts. For instance, one of the minitheories of project management predicts a project's doom if PM practitioners do not complete it on time, on budget, and maintain quality. PM practitioners also use these theoretical underpinnings to determine success and failure (Project Management Institute [PMI], 2013; Connelly, 2014). What impairs the relationship between theory and research is a lack of compatibility between the research question or hypothesis and the theoretical foundation of phenomena.

Sharma (2013) and Swanson and Chermack (2013) indicated that an incomplete, nebulous, and parochial theory is destructive to good practice. They explained that most researchers erroneously limit theoretical development to hypothesis testing instead of confirming and refining conceptualization, constricting the process by applying qualitative or quantitative and feminist points of view or methodologies. Swanson and Chermack (2013) recommended three essential criteria for theory building: the purpose, the intended boundary, and the cohesion. Boundaries are the contexts or locations within which the theory occurs or operates. The cohesion connects the constructs and elements, purpose, content, and how the theory will be measured or assessed.

The Application of Research Methods in Theory Development

Universally, there are three categories of theoretical methods that researchers use to gather facts, data, and evidence to test or verify assumptions, propositions, and research questions about phenomena and contribute to developing theories. They are quantitative, qualitative, and mixed methods. These methods use various instruments to gather data, including surveys, interviews, library research, focus group, observation, video recording, and archival research, to name a few. Each contributes uniquely to the process of theory development.

These research methods' common goal is to ensure transparency and freedom from endogenous and exogenous biases that may confound and threaten the research results' trustworthiness and generalizability (Gilstrap, 2013; Vogt et al., 2012; Thomas et al., 2014; Yoshikawa et al., 2013).

Researchers use quantitative and qualitative methods or a combination of both to discover the meanings of phenomena and contribute to the development of theory. Both methodologies gather data from surveys, interviews, and focus groups. Ontological and epistemological differences, however, exist between them. While qualitative methods describe, interprets, verifies, and evaluates phenomena, the qualitative method is inductive and subjective.

On the other hand, the quantitative method seeks knowledge through deductive, empirical, mathematical, and objective means. It measures cause and effect relationships between or among variables. Both methodologies are susceptible to various criticisms. Subjective realities are more likely to contain errors of judgment. Equally, striving for objective realities through a cause-and-effect relationship in a nonlinear, uncertain, and complex world of project management can be elusive, if not impossible (Yoshikawa et al., 2013). Researchers use qualitative and quantitative research methodologies to contribute to theory development. Through mixed methodologies, a researcher can combine quantitative and qualitative methods to achieve the research goals. The researcher applies quantitative research methods to gather data through various instruments, including probability sampling, surveys, interviews, and discussions.

Qualitative research design methodology's tools are case study, ethnographic studies, phenomenological studies, grounded theory, and content analysis. The researchers use inductive, interpretative, and open-ended strategies to have a thorough understanding of phenomena (Vogt et al., 2012). Observational studies, correlational research, developmental designs, longitudinal, developmental studies, and survey research constitute quantitative research methodologies (Gilstrap, 2013; Thomas et al., 2014). The quantitative method is deductive and uses numbers to analyze data. This allows the quantitative research method to generalize, predict, and determine cause-and-effect relationships between variables.

The use of the quantitative method enables the use of numbers and statistical software to analyze and report the research data results. The process and the results can be objective and seamlessly repeated by a third researcher (Yilmaz, 2013). On the other hand, a qualitative method empowers the researcher to analyze data and report the results. This makes the application of the qualitative method subjective. Hirshon et al. (2013) indicated that the qualitative method employs open-ended questions, explains in detail participants' feelings, experiences, and thoughts, obtains data through structured and nonstructured interviews, focus groups, and narratives. This makes the qualitative method detail-oriented when it comes to data gathering. The hybrid methods use qualitative and quantitative methods (Gilstrap, 2013; Vogt et al., 2012; Thomas et al., 2014; Yoshikawa et al., 2013). This gives the mixed methods more research power, especially its ability to juxtapose and triangulate data from multiple sources.

This study's research design is based on a multiple-case study, a qualitative research design methodology. A case study is a careful and in-depth study of a social unit such as an individual, event, neighborhood, school, corporation, or division within a corporation that attempts to determine what factors led to its success or failure. A case study can provide the opportunity to learn or expose the works and life of an individual or institution that was never known or studied. It also enables researchers to gather comprehensive data and make detailed records of the event, including social, historical, economic, physical, and environmental factors that influence the case study. The data gathered during the case study are specific, categorized, identified in patterns, synthesized, and generalized.

Furthermore, in the conduct of a case study, researchers analyze data in various ways, including organizing comprehensive information about the case, categorizing the data, interpreting events, identifying common patterns, synthesizing, and generalizing the results (Leedy and Ormrod, 2013; Yin, 2014). The case report generally includes the rationale of the study, a detailed description of the facts related to the case, a description of the data collected, a discussion of the patterns found, and the large scheme of things (Yin, 2014).

Data will be gathered from several projects, programs, and globally based organizations within one or serval North American countries. This method will compare what is unique, homogenous, and heterogeneous about PM current theory and PMT 2.0. The result from the discovery will determine the level of contribution to the development of theory. Ellis and Levy (2008), Naor et al. (2013), and Wacker (1998) agreed on a set of criteria that can be used to evaluate the theory. The essential elements are definition (what and who), domain limitation (when and where), relationship building (why and how), and predictive assumptions (could, should, and would).

The project management field is being expanded rapidly due to projectification, programmification, and globalization efforts. Any research that intends to contribute in a meaningful or significant way to theory in this domain must consider the linear (deterministic and inductive) and nonlinear (holistic and deductive) dimensions that result from these expansions. If deductive, the researcher may start with a hypothesis intended to test cause and effect relationships between variables, such as traditional and modern project management methodologies. In the inductive case, the researcher starts with an observation and questions and builds the data theory (Ellis and Levy, 2008). Harlow (2009) and Stam (1998, 2000, 2006) indicated a symbiotic relationship between research data and theory and that expanding our understanding of data leads to a theory. Understanding PM's complex nature helps the researcher cogently define and explain the phenomena and accurately predict events based on conceptual foundations.

The research contributes to theory through methods specific to three categories as follows: (a) analytical, conceptual research, (b) case study, and (c) empirical statistical research. The application of multiple-case studies is propitious to build theory. Harlow (2009), Stam (1996, 2000, 2006), and (Wacker 1998) acknowledged the significance of case studies in contributing to theory development. They explained that a case study could disprove the viability of an existing theory and, therefore, can potentially contribute to theory building through empirical evidence and testing. Studies show that theory development and testing are interconnected (Harlow, 2010). Through retroduction, a researcher can retest a theory when a new set of data is discovered that can determine whether the new discovery is significant enough to replace the existing theory. A theory can be expanded by interpreting new realities or facts gathered through interviews, surveys, discussions, or seminars. Harlow (2009, 2010) stated that the process of theory development is recursive or cyclical: the researcher can gather data through observations, surveys. If the data fail to validate the theory, the researcher can reject the research or place a moratorium on it and start an entirely new project. However, if the data provide sufficient empirical evidence to invalidate the current theory, a new theory is espoused.

The analytical, conceptual research method encourages creativity, innovation, and organization of concepts or constructs. It creates internally consistent logical relationships among complex and abstract concepts. Like an empirical case study, this method gathers data through a case study as evidence to validate what the researcher assumes about these conceptualizations. The researcher can draw information or ideas from experience, conceptual modeling, and hermeneutics, i.e., interpretation or deduction of facts from observation to develop theory. Empirical, experimental design examines and tests performances, differences among the old and new theory, including the cause-and-effect relationships among variables or constructs, some of which can be direct or indirect, endogenous or exogenous (Solaiman et al., 2016). By putting in place some control mechanism, the research investigators can test whether projectification, programmification, and globalization have created a significant mismatch or epistemological gap between current project management theory and the complex and nonlinear realities of the project management domain.

The Impact of PPGE on Industries

During the last decade, organizations outsourced PM and IT services to fulfill specific organizational strategies: to accelerate the process of bringing goods and services to market faster by effectively controlling cost, reducing red tape, and meeting quality requirements (Packendorf and Lindgren, 2013). The continued dismal failures of the return rate on capital, coupled with the economic recession, rigorous regulatory requirements, challenges of globalization, and the toughening of the competitive climate, have compelled most industries to integrate PM temporary services perennial organization operations. However, these mammoth organizational shifts are not entirely aligned or consistent with PM's current theory, which does not fully describe, explain, and predict the relationships among manifold and interconnected variables and constructs. Studies conducted in the United Kingdom, Canada, and Austria pointed out that the application of PM's trilogy is not adequate to predict the performance of scope, cost, and time in a PPGE-based-complex, interrelated and interdependent-project environment (Gransberg et al., 2013; Kiridena and Sense, 2016). Packendorf and Lindgren (2013) indicated that making project management influence and control the PPGE-based organizations constitutes a significant organizational change and should be recognized by social science communities. In other words, the upsurge of the impact of projectification, programmification, and globalization endeavors integrate not only the operation of a permanent organization and a PM temporary function but present grave multidimensional challenges to PM practitioners. Some of these challenges include internal and external competitions, trade wars, currency manipulation, industrial espionage activities, data breaches, cyber warfare, legal, socioeconomic, cultural, and linguistic differences. There are also ethical and social issues that have the potential to derail organizational operations. PM practitioners and organizational leaders wishing to work in foreign countries have onerous, multifaceted tasks to perform: to make their business profitable and distance themselves from acts that the US government considers illegal and unethical. In a globalized milieu, knowledge of PM phenomena' interconnected, complex, and risky nature is a survival strategy; no one is insulated or inviolated. A collapse of an institution due to bad institutional policies or a group of internal or external economic and political disruptors can have domino effects on the rest of the world. Negrea (2012) noted that PPGE efforts could augment trade activities such as capital flow and investment activities. They can also integrate national economic systems, remove trade barriers, tariffs, and protectionism. Battistuzzo and Piscopo (2015) added that to operate an overseas project or business exposes a managing team to a gamut of factors, including liability, cultural issues, and understanding theory can guide practitioners to predict the behavior of events and can enhance the success of organizational activities. Since a theory does not exist in a vacuum, the study will use construction, education, health care, information technology (IT), management, pharmaceutical, and transportation industries. To illustrate the complexity of managing PPGE-based projects and how applying a good and virtuous theory is propitious to sustainable endeavors. The participants in this dissertation study will be purposely selected from these industries; they exemplify the complexity, nonlinearity, and uncertainty due to PPGE efforts. They also represent a microcosm of projects managed across frontiers. Moreover, data gathered from these industries will have the chance to be replicated and generalized to other PPGE-based, mega, or complex projects across different sectors. Compared to the extant PM theory, PMT 2.0 will help organizations and PM practitioners understand and subsequently predict the relationships among the plethora of interconnected and interdependent concepts and constructs.

Construction

The construction industry is pervasive and thus attractive to investors and aspiring entrepreneurs. It is, however, capital intensive, and the risk associated with workplace safety, including the social cost of construction on the environment and communities, can be high (Celik et al., 2017). The industry is also vulnerable to cost overruns, schedule delays, and poor scope management (Jallow et al., 2014). To thrive internationally requires understanding cultural differences, market fluctuation, hyper-competition, internal and external regulations, economic vicissitudes, corrupt regimes, and the gusto and tenacity to work within extraneous and culturally incompatible, and sometimes hostile terrains.

Moreover, to achieve success, management must deal with multiple legal and ethical standards. Management must also deal with labor-management relations, sexual harassment, employee health and safety, employment discrimination, child labor, the Uniform Commercial Code, and contract management, to name a few. Jallow et al. (2014) noted that construction projects' complexity could be exemplified by complex drawings, project specifications, and the throng of contractors, subcontractors, and seasonal workers that they manage quotidianly.

Keeping vigil on these interrelated, interdependent, and complex factors is onerous. Studies show that laser focusing mainly on copes, schedule, cost overruns is no longer tenable in achieving complex projects' goals (Qasi et al., 2016; Williams, 2015). Complexity causes unknowns and unknowns to increase, and when an organization decides to operate globally, those risks multiply astronomically. Bakhshi et al. (2016) indicated that projects are becoming increasingly complex due to emergent neonisms such as projectification, programmification, and globalization. These intricate neologisms, they explained, can no longer be separated from PM ethos. Disengaging from or blatantly ignoring discussion on these complex phenomena will continue to debase efforts required to achieve success in managing complex projects fully. PMT 2.0 is being developed to describe, explain, and provide PM and organizational personnel the tools they need to predict these constructs' behaviors and interactions and achieve sustainable success. Ayayi et al. (2016) noted that when construction practitioners adhere strictly to theory and project drawings and avoid creeping the project's scope, construction waste and rework can be minimized.

Education

The debate about teaching PM courses and using PM-proven concepts, tools, and standards to manage educational activities persist.

The demand for certified PM professionals to deliver products and services most expeditiously has spurred increasing interest in teaching PM at educational institutions of higher learning. PM's teaching is also encouraged; both public and private organizational leaders agreed that project management's effective implementation could drive society's socioeconomic development and growth (Dimitri, 2013). Louw et al. (2012) and Saungweme (2015) reported that developing and expanding the study of project management in all university curricula in South Africa, for instance, will provide sufficient training to PM practitioners and will develop skills and capabilities in PM knowledge areas. This will keep pace with the demand for well-balanced and qualified project managers. Thomas et al. (2008) and Albrecht et al. (2014) underscored the significance of project management education and the complex nature of projects which project management practitioners handle daily. Using project management methodology and PMBK 10 knowledge areas, Thomas et al. (2008) and Albrecht et al. (2014) took a new look at an advanced level of training and skill-building in project management, including the examination of virtual project management and the creation of an extended learning environment for project management practitioners. Thomas et al. (2008) also indicated that entry-level project management is no longer sufficient to address the ever-increasing complex nature of project management. The alarming rate of project completion fiascos, they claimed, is due to the lower level of traditional learning paradigm based on instruction and training instead of developing master managers adaptive and responsive in working and collaborating with diverse interests in a virtual setting. Ally et al. (2010) indicated that through the application of advanced levels of collaborative technology, such as teleworking, high institutions of learning across the globe are managing complex projects online and providing PM training opportunities to students and working adults. Alves et al. 2016 and Saungweme (2015) also reported that the application of project-based learning (PBL) methodology is used in many educational institutions to develop interest and motivation in technical and transversal skills in engineering programs.

PBL also encourages students to plan and execute projects and find tangible solutions to real-world problems. Instead of a student-focus curriculum by which students are instructed via multiple channels, including classroom instruction, media presentation, video platforms, PBL's curriculum is project-based. It integrates theory and practice, student and community interests, public and private business concerns, and parent and school management supports (Smith and Gibson, 2016). Liu (2016) indicated that PBL encourages learning; it facilitates access to training facilities online. Studies show that the appropriate way to alter the course of continuous project failure is to invest in training and educate tomorrow's project leaders (Ramazani and Jergeas, 2014). According to Ramazani and Jergeas (2014) and Valle and Lanier (2016), the nature of such training and educating should focus on training students and trainees to understand complex projects and develop interpersonal, leadership, and soft skills and practice project management in real-life scenarios.

Johnson et al. (2015) believed that macro training programs in PM change corporate culture and environment because a learning culture breeds creativity and innovations. It empowers an organization to thrive. They also indicated that advanced project leadership training expands organizational abilities, builds lucrative relationships, and contributes immensely to achieving overarching corporate objectives. In other words, when people who are supposed to make decisions have superior skills, they are bound to make better and well-calculated decisions (Maltzman and Shirley, 2010). Moreover, since a well-trained workforce is adaptable and better ready to meet the global business climate's competitive nature, most fortune 500 organizations invest enormous resources in Rand D and training programs; it makes an organization competitive. Studies show that businesses and projects succeed when leaders perform effectively (Nixon et al., 2011).

Contrary to the extant PM theory, PMT 2.0 espouses the notion that knowledge workers are game changers. They can alter an environment from incubating project mortality (failure) to immortality (sustainability). In other words, the more knowledgeable one becomes of PM complex phenomena, the better the chance to achieve sustainable success.

Health Care

The health care industry is undergoing dramatic changes regarding patient care support and the costs of achieving organizational objectives. Organizations, including those involved in the health care supply chain process, are pressured by regulations, politicians, and a throng of individuals and special interest groups to deliver health care services expeditiously at a lower price, expand access to everyone, and simultaneously maintain quality service. To survive, health care organizations have opted to integrate health care delivery systems by various means, including mergers, acquisitions, projects, programs, and portfolio management. The integration of incompatible concepts such as PM temporality and organizations that operate permanently has made the health care industry complex, robust and monolithic. To create and implement strategic decisions requires input from multiple actors and interest groups with dissimilar interests. Anthropoulos et al. (2015), Batkins and Brannon (2014), Boardman et al. (2016), and Venkatesh et al. (2014) indicated that complex organizations are uncertain, nonlinear, and chaotic. Traditional PM concepts such as trilogy and a project's lifecycle will not thrive in such a complex milieu. Without any theoretical guidance to provide the road map that practitioners, division, and department leaders need to understand these complexities and endeavor to predict the success and failure of what they pursue or undertake, the results of their actions will indeed become susceptible and vulnerable to fortuity.

Information Technology

For practical and theoretical purposes, the field of project management is associated with information technology. Through the application of PM tools, standards, and theory, IT professionals, including software developers across frontiers, have made the IT field ubiquitous and sine qua non to business or organization success worldwide. Information technology helps an organization provide products and services faster at a competitive price. IT projects have also continued to develop nodes and data processing software systems to assist organizations in achieving their tactical and strategic objectives. Moyland et al. (2015) noted that the advancement in information technology and telecommunication systems had created new software and hardware, including smartphones, tablets, digital audio recorders, and Computer-Assisted Qualitative Data Analysis Software (CAQDAS). CAQDAS helps researchers organize better, manage, analyze, and calculate data especially numerical data, faster and accurately.

Moreover, Terlizzi et al. (2015) reported that financial organizations in Brazil, for instance, spent US$351 billion in 2014 on IT management, and the country has made concerted efforts to institutionalize the application of project management methodology considered a panacea to success across industries in the country. Despite the enormous investment in IT projects, Wells (2012) indicated an alignment problem between IT projects and the parent organization's objective, adversely impacting stakeholders' anticipated project benefits. PPGE's institutionalization has made interaction and share of project data expeditiously among staffers and managers across multiple frontiers. It has also minimized or eliminated the hurdles involved in protecting intellectual property (IP) rights overseas and the misaligned and disjoint relationships that heretofore existed between outsourced IT projects and their parent organizations. Stone et al. (2015) indicated that, unlike in the past, IT personnel were impersonal and lacked interpersonal skills. Through PPGE efforts, IT managers, developers, and evangelists have learned to work in a global environment connecting with stakeholders' clients. Wagner et al. (2014) developed a new capital social theory to foster an operation alignment, including informal relationships, interactions, mutual trust, and shared language, between IT management executives and business enterprises. They believed that social interactions exerted influence on the extent to which IT managers and businesses can align. Social interactions include understanding informal relation-ships and sharing common cognitive values.

IT has also become an effective tool to breach data, engage in industrialize espionage activities and cyber warfare. Due to the high rate of risk and uncertainty in an IT project's success, business orga-nizations are inclining toward merging or insourcing PM activities and functions along with the data-to-day operations of the parent organization. Studies show that integrating PM and organization functions in a globalized business environment makes the PM field bigger. A tangible solution to PM low output will continue to be elusive if the PM current theory does not fully explain, describe, and predict these constructs' relationships. Wiener et al. (2016) indicated that software prototypes, artifacts, inconsistent and incompatible objectives among manifold stakeholders, along with the volatility of IT, continue to deepen the complexity and uncertainty of IT proj-ects. The frequency of data breaches and identity crimes is further raising concern and compelling stakeholders to look elsewhere for solutions that remain elusive (Stone et al., 2015)

Management

Public and private management hierarchies embrace projectifi-cation and programmification concepts and investigate the need to integrate them into how organizations or businesses operate or func-tion. Experts and connoisseurs in organization management have little doubt that PPGE efforts will remedy the traditional PM's low performance and its continuous failure to maximize capital return. The Fed and the European Union consider projectification and pro-grammification to be cost-cutting and bureaucratic reduction tools. The United States National Academy of Public Administration [The Academy] (2015) plans to apply the time-tested project management and program management tools to manage programs, incredibly complex programs. The Academy believes that well-trained PM pro-fessionals can manage complex projects in the most cost-effective and administratively effective manner; programmification has demonstrated successes across various industries and organizations-private, and the public. It has been estimated that the Fed will save over $995 billion by 2025 through programmification and projectification efforts. In a decade, an estimate of Asian infrastructure expansion projects is expected to surpass $8 trillion (Lu et al., 2015).

Profound ontological and epistemological gaps exist between PM temporary functions and permanent business management operations. In other words, which methodology or theory will dominate the PM integrated zone, the PM theory of temporality or perennial organizational operation? How will PM management relinquish its traditional functions of setting strategic goals and mobilizing resources, planning, organizing, controlling, and coordinating multiple tasks to achieve those objectives? What will become of the PM trilogy, project lifecycle, and PMBOK Knowledge Areas? Will PM lose its temporality and identity as an independent field of study? Certainty, PPGE efforts have expanded PM territorial domain more than its capacity to explain, to practitioners, the answers to these questions and predict the relationships among PPGE conceptualizations.

Pharmaceutics

The increase in regulatory compliance, competitive and political pressure, the shift in the aging population, and income disparity have led this industry to integrate PM and program concepts and its management. The PM and program-proven tools such as strategic planning and portfolio management effectively curb the risk of developing drugs and investing only on a portfolio of projects with the potential of short and long-term profitability (Kaiser et al., 2014; Rijke et al., 2014).

Miterev et al. (2015) indicated that program managers' various skillsets could determine the pharmaceutical industry's success and failure rate. They explained that a program manager's competency level influences programs' success and that transferrable skill sets such as leadership and communication are essential regardless of the program type. They also indicated that certain types of programs require a collection of different competencies and proposed that program management may need a contingency tool to match certain programs to a specific skill set.

Transportation

The transportation industry is vast, pervasive, complex, and associated with complex procurement. It is made up of the ground, air, and water carriers. Besides military aircraft, customer service is at the core of the transportation industry, especially passenger aircraft, trains, buses, trucks, and cars, to name few examples. Love et al. (2016) indicated that the need to invest in transportation infrastructure could not be overemphasized; the construction of additional or broader roads, bridges, and railways is needed in response to the growth of national demographics. Better transportation channels are also required to meet the 21st-century market challenges and competitiveness of globalization. Despite the application of traditional project management concepts, cost overruns in the transportation field are exponentially rising. Studies show that part of the rise in cost overrun is due to the complexity of managing transportation projects (Nguyen et al., 2014; Qureshi and Kang, 2014).

Gransberg et al. (2013) advised project portfolio management to rank projects because of their value and learned to let go of risk-ridden projects. Sciara et al. (2016) indicated that transportation complexity includes a federal mandate to conserve and restore natural resources when new roads are constructed and mitigate the impact of ecological degradation on habitats and other species. They explained that transportation agencies now run multiple programs simultaneously instead of handling one project at a time. This enables the transportation industry in the United States to assess and evaluate environmental impact and mitigation costs and compare outcomes before making decisions.

Wilman (2016) noted that the transportation industry's programmification and projectification improve performance and customer service and enhance revenue management. She explained that a skillful program or project serves customers quickly and effectively, reduces time spent loading and unloading luggage, and manages seasonal fluctuations professionally. Globalization and advancement in technology and rigid regulatory standards, and product inspection have increased product recalls. However, Kalaignanam et al. (2013) indicated that automobile recall improves public safety and reduces fatality. These product recalls impact stakeholders, including customers, and can erode their confidence and trust in the industry. Bowen and Zheng (2014) divulged how Toyota's 3.4 million vehicle recall damaged its reputation and severely and negatively impacted stakeholders in that company.

Nguyen et al. (2014) and Qureshi and Kang (2014) asserted that complex technological factors could increase the risks involved in implementing projects. They increase project risks. Thamhain (2013) and Verweij (2014) indicated that it requires stakeholders' commitment and its parts for a complex project to achieve its goals. It also requires public and private partnerships. Organizational factors can snowball and adversely affect the other elements. Managing these complexities requires guidance, a system of thought, and a theory that can fully explain and predict these interconnected and interdependent constructs' relationship outcomes. The application of program and portfolio management, they claimed, enables project and program managers to identify transportation projects from the complexity perspectives and the cost of managing complex projects.

Summary

The use of scholarly and peer-reviewed articles and journals in this dissertation research will bolster and guide the researcher's effort to pose the right questions. Empirical evidence was gathered from multiple sources in developing a new PM theory 2.0 (PMT2.0) and exploring the similarities and dissimilarities between the extant PM theory and the emergent PMT2.0.

Due to philosophical and theoretical reasons, a standard definition of theory is yet to be achieved. Studies show that a multiple-case study method can develop a new theory via empirical evidence. It also guides the researcher in obtaining suitable answers to research questions (Yin, 2014). The PPGE has expanded the project management field more than its extant theory can describe, explain, and predict.

Key industries such as construction, education, IT, health care, management, pharmaceutics, and transportation have become complex to manage due to PPGE efforts (Godenhjelm et al., 2014). The lack of understanding of the effect of PPGE efforts has also placed PM and IT methodologies in a dilemma: While they have striven to make headway in the software industry, mainly in an onsite environment, they must ask themselves some tough questions. How will software developers and teams learn to work with larger multinational teams across national boundaries? How prepared do they understand the complexity, chaos and concomitantly meet or exceed disparate stakeholders' expectations? The answers to these questions may unravel some of the uncertainties, challenges, sophistication, and confusion that PPGE efforts have established (Nguyen et al., 2014; Qureshi and Kang, 2014).

Without a good and virtuous theory that will guide practitioners to understand these complex phenomena, tangible solutions will continue to be elusive (Gelso, 2006; Wacker, 1998). Further, the integration of permanent management operation and PM temporal function is paradoxical. Without knowing the marriage's complexity between temporality and permanence, PM practitioners may be incapable of predicting PM activities' success or failure. PM may also stand to lose its innovative and competitive edge. In other words, there is a mismatched or misaligned relationship that exists between the present PM theory and what the PM domain has become due to PPGE efforts (Bergman et al., 2013; Maranon and Pera, 2015).

PMT 2.0 was developed to fill that epistemological gap-to provide a complete definition, description, and prediction of the current PM realities. PMT 2.0 espouses the notion that knowledge workers can change the game between a project's mortality (chaos, uncertainty, nonlinearity, and complexity) and immortality (sustainability, success, and maximizing the return of capital) (Godenhjelm et al., 2014). Data gathered will be analyzed and compared. Four theoretical criteria and good theory virtues were used to evaluate PM extant theory and the PMT 2.0 (Gelso, 2006; Wacker, 1998).

CHAPTER 3

Research Method

The projectification, programmification, and globalization escalation (PPGE) integrate permanent organizational operations and PM impermanent functions (Artto et al., 2015; Lindsey et al., 2016). Godenhjelm et al. (2014) argued that PPGE increases a project's environmental, legal, political, socioeconomic, and entrepreneurial constructs and complexities beyond the current project management theoretical capacity to fully describe, explain, and predict the behavior success, or failure of these complex phenomena. PM theory's inability to keep pace with these complex realities has created an epistemological gap between the current PM theory and what the PM domain has become due to PPGE (Bergman et al., 2013; Maranon and Pera, 2015). This hiatus has added to the litany of PM's pathologies. Over 60 percent of megaprojects fail (Fein, 2012). Worldwide annual investment in MP falls between $6 to $9 trillion (Flyvbjerg, 2014).

The purpose of this multiple-case study was twofold: to develop a new PM theory 2.0 (PMT2.0) that will be compatible with and aligned with what the PM domain has become due to PPGE and to explore and compare the extant PM theory and the PMT2.0. Empirical evidence gathered from observations, interviews, strategic organizational reports, and archives were compared to determine if PPGE had expanded the PM domain's theoretical base, whether PPGE affected PM success, and which theory (the extant or the new) was superior. The extent of the study's contribution to knowledge will depend on stakeholders' conformity to the utility, relevance to PM phenomena, and superiority of PMT 2.0 after the publication of the research findings. PMT2.0 will provide a holistic theoretical perspective of the PM domain. Furthermore, PMT2.0 can explain, describe, and predict the chaos, complexity, nonlinearity, uncertainty that PPGE poses to project management. (Bergman et al., 2013; Maranon and Pera, 2015). The independent constructs are programmification, projectification, globalization, and project-based organization. The dependent constructs are PM theory, PM domain, project failure, knowledge of PM phenomena, and project success. The population sample was purposely limited to PMI chapters across North America, Europe, Asia Pacific, the Middle East, Africa, Latin America, and PM practitioners associated with the International Project Management Association (IPMA). Participating units of analysis will comprise construction, education, health care, information technology (IT), management, pharmaceutical, and transportation industries.

Research Questions

The research questions focused on obtaining empirical evidence required to achieve the purposes of developing a new PM theory 2.0 (PMT2.0) and exploring the similarities and dissimilarities between the extant PM theory and the PMT2.0. The study sought answers to the following questions:

RQ1. How do PPGE efforts broaden the scope of the PM domain and impact the application of PM theory?

RQ2. How do PPGE efforts limit the current PM theory's capacity to fully describe, explain, and predict complex, uncertain, and nonlinear phenomena?

RQ3. How do a complete understanding, description, and prediction of complex, uncertain, and nonlinear phenomena impact a project's success?

RQ4. How do PPGE efforts transform the PM domain and its theory?

RQ5. How do these transformational efforts impact or influence PM theory and practice?

RQ6. How does the development of a new PM theory (the proposed PMT 2.0, for example) eliminate the gap between PM extant theory and the expansion of the project management domain due to PPGE?

RQ7. What challenges have PM practitioners experienced due to PPGE efforts?

Research Methods and Design

A multiple-case study will apply in conducting the research. It uses words as data for analysis rather than numbers that the quantitative method pursues. These data will come from participants' feelings, idiosyncrasies, experiences, belief systems, and archives (McKusker and Gunaydin, 2015). Baxter and Jack (2008) and Yin (2003) recommended the use of a multiple-case study method when the purpose of the study is to seek answers to the who, why, and how questions (Baxter and Jack, 2008; Yin, 2003). Studies show that a multiple-case study method is propitious to developing a theory (Park and Park, 2016; Vishual, 2012). The use of a multiple case study can also make the research theoretically replicable, transferrable, and predictable. It compares units or participants across various locations (Yin, 2003). This increases the generalizability of the research results. A multiple-case study procedure comprises the following phases: (a) planning the research, (b) selecting the cases, (c) designing the study protocol, (d) collecting the data, (e) analyzing and interpreting the data, and (f) reporting the findings (De Massis and Kotlar, 2014; Yin, 2014)

Plan the Research

Key issues involved in the research planning stage included reading the literature, identifying the research interest or problem, crafting the topic, and formulating the research questions and propositions. A well-formed problem statement contains the following components: What, who, how, where, when, and why.

The what asserts the problem, including something that is going on that is wrong or disappointing, that the researcher is concerned about and intends to find a solution. The who constitutes scholarly references, peer-review materials, experts, or prevailing views of the field of project management that have provided support for and acknowledgment of the problem's existence. The how, where, and when describes the situation both negatively and positively. The where pinpoints the location where the problem's impact seems apparent. The who contains a list of peer-reviewed references that provide support for the situation that the research tries to solve and describe the problem's nature. Why identifies the theoretical framework of the problem under study and what other writers or researchers say is the cause of the problem (Ellis and Levy, 2008).

Identify the Population.

The second phase is to identify the population-case units or participants from which the empirical data will be drawn or solicited. The units of analysis can be organizations, schools, cities, states or municipalities, or individuals. The study asked approximately 112 PM practitioners to participate in the research. They were chosen from seven major PM industries, including construction, education, health care, information technology (IT), management, pharmaceutics, and transportation.

Design the Instruments and Protocols

The next phase will govern the conduct and implementation of the research. It defines the research field procedures, the type of data to collect, and the relationship between interview or survey questions and the data (Yin, 2012, 2014). Studies show that a multiple case study is complex; it entails meeting deadlines, complying with legal and ethical considerations, and using various media to reach participants. Identifying the right instruments to use and establishing a set of guidelines or protocols to guide the entire research can minimize or eliminate ethical and procedural risks. Instruments or data collection methods include observation, interview, survey, archival, and documentation. The multiplicity of the research instruments fosters triangulation and increases the strengths of the research. Risks may occur if the research instrument was not designed correctly or if participants were not told what the research was trying to achieve (see Appendix A). Studies show that a well-crafted and detailed research protocol can determine scientific research's success (Eisenhardt, 2011; Yin, 2012, 2014).

Analyze the Data

This phase of the research entails organizing, juxtaposing, and coding data. It also includes redaction, translation, and transcription. An essential part of data analysis is identifying cross-case patterns. Identifying common patterns across case studies will also facilitate understanding the disparity among the seven units of analysis composed of construction, education, health care, information technology (IT), management, pharmaceutical, and transportation. A common pattern also supports connectivity, relationship, and interconnectedness among the constructs or variables. Further, it determines the opposite effect if there are unusual patterns among the constructs (Simons, 2012).

Reporting the Findings

The research study followed credibility, transferability, dependability, reliability, and confirmability standards to gauge trustworthy findings. The research study also applied those standards to judge and evaluate common patterns in the interview data. The credibility determines if the impact of the relationships among the constructs and variables is positive or negative. Dependability checks whether the logical links between PM extant theory and PMT 2.0 emergent theory and their constructs operate correctly. Transferability examines how exogenous factors such as external economic, political, legal, environmental, and cultural constraints impact the theoretical domain. Reliability explores how the study can be replicated or repeated to produce the same results. Confirmability indicates that the empirical evidence is inextricably linked to the data, that the findings fully represent what is being researched, and that the reader finds the results adequately verifiable (De Massis and Kotlar, 2014; Yin, 2014).

A set of propositions and research questions will guide the research. Data and empirical evidence will be gathered through various instruments, including surveys, interviews, observation, opinions, narratives, and participants' views. Surveys and interviews will be conducted via computer-aided programs and face-to-face. Moreover, the four theoretical elements, including the eight virtues of theoretical criteria, will be used to evaluate and compare the extant PM theory and PMT2.0. The four elements are conceptual definition, domain limitations, relationship-building, and predictions. The current and emergent PM theories were evaluated based on the following eight theoretical virtues: uniqueness, parsimony, conservatism, generalizability, fecundity, internal consistency, empirical riskiness, and abstraction (Wacker,1998, 2004). A well-thought-out and written protocol followed the road map and guided the research's management through the four phraseologies. Salient among the key protocol issues are the research study design, quality and implementation of questionnaires, surveys, interviews, ethical issues, recording, transcription, type of hardware, and software.

Populations/Sample

A total of 112 sampling participants will be purposively selected to participate in the study. There will be PPGE-based units (N =56). 8 participants will be selected from each of seven industries: construction, transportation, health care, IT, pharmaceutical, education, and management (Eriksson and Kovalainen, 2012). Equally, the researcher will select PM practitioners (N = 56) from PPGE-based PM organizations. The unit organizations and PM practitioners will be selected from various PMI chapter-based geographic regions. There will be eight units from North America, eight from South America, eight from Europe, eight from the Asia Pacific, and eight from the Middle East and Africa. The geographic dispersion of the sample will increase the generalizability of the research. The ages of participants and their years of experience will be 24 and sixth months, respectively.

The choice of this geographic dispersion and the size of selected sampling participants will ensure equivalency and illuminate an in-depth discourse from different angles and PM sectors on the impact of PPGE on the PM domain across frontiers. Moreover, the knowledge of or applying the Project Management Guide Book (PMBOK) is common among PM practitioners, including PMI chapter members worldwide. This shared knowledge will make a replication strategy practical and feasible. Studies show that the more significant or broader the population's representative sample, the greater the research results' reliability (Field, 2013; Yin, 2014).

Materials/Instrumentation

The study will primarily use Google Survey, SurveyMonkey, Facebook, LinkedIn, and Twitter to disseminate information about the dissertation research study. Studies show that there are approximately two billion social media users. Social network sites have become de facto platforms for research and information sharing across geopolitical boundaries (Haynes, Bawden, and Robinson, 2016; Manca and Ranieri, 2016). Approximately 101 participants will complete the online open-ended interview questions. Only 11 participants will be phone or face-to-face interviewed, conducted mainly in the North American region.

The study will snowball the sampling on other professional networks or social media sites to recruit PMI chapter members worldwide. PMI membership soared to 51 million in 2013 (Project Management Institute [PMI], 2013). PMI also has over 150 chapters established in 50 US states, including Puerto Rico (PMI.org). The study will ask a total of 14 questions organized into seven categories (see Appendix E). Audiotapes notes, and follow-up surveys, and phone calls will be used in the interview process. Interviews may be restaged to verify conflicting information or inadequate response to essential questions (Padgett, 2004).

The average interview time will be approximately 35 minutes. Some management protocols such as time limit and mechanics of conducting and implementing the interviews may be altered from site to site, case unit to case unit, or participant to participant. This is based on the dictate of what may transpire in the process.

Study Procedures

The study will diligently follow the paragon procedures and standards that Northcentral University (NCU), Institutional Review Board (IRB), and the conduct of multiple-case study method have ascribed, sanctioned, and encouraged. NCU sets a high Academic Integrity Policy standard for dissertation researchers and has a zero-tolerance policy toward plagiarism, an unauthorized act of taking or using someone else's work including but not limited to writing, art, graphics, photos, images, and tables without crediting or citing the source in the manner appropriate to the scientific community.

NCU also guides candidates conducting dissertation research to understand various ethical standards, including the APA Ethical code, the Nuremberg Code, the Declaration of Helsinki, and the Belmont Report. Knowledge of the law and research ethics are integral in extirpating errors, mistakes, negligence, and intellectual dishonesty. The research will minimize behaviors and actions that could compromise the Hippocratic Oath and exploit others. NCU also makes it mandatory to use various successfully proven tools and templates, peer review literature, and the highest analytical skills to conduct and implement a research project. IRB has a mandate and vested interest in ensuring the implementation of research without chicanery and deception. Participants, especially children, prisoners, mentally ill, or uneducated people, are treated humanely and without harm. The IRB safeguards the adherence to and application of the Informed Consent procedure and conflicts of interest (Committee on Science, Engineering, and Public Policy, 2009).

Before officially scheduling an interview with potential human subjects, the study will obtain a complete informed consent agreement from each participant. Participants will have full access to these pieces of information, including a list of contacts that they can call or email if they have cold feet, want to withdraw from the research, or intend to seek additional information.

In conformity with NCU and IRB standards, the research will safeguard participants' privacy and confidentiality and data recorded and stored during the course. After the research, they will be protected from third-party access and destroyed based on IRB requirements (APA, 2010). Rev.com will be hired to transcribe audio and video recordings. ATLAS.ti 8 software will also be used to transcribe the same data audio and video sources.

Transcription, raw data collection, and analysis will occur concurrently. This will help collect new data if the existing empirical evidence is deemed less critical. Transcription triangulation will boost the research validity. ATLAS.ti 8 software will be used to organize text, audio, and video files. It can also query specific information that may require additional interrogation. The qualitative research software can also map concepts and data, visualize charts or ideas, and aid the generation of reports (Friese, 2014).

Data Collection and Analysis

Data collection and analysis achieve two primary goals, namely, to gather and analyze empirical data. The collection process consists of using the design instruments (interview questions, surveys, questionnaires, software, and hardware) to gather evidence from those selected to participate in the research. The study will employ a semi-structured interview format. The data's management, analysis, and safeguards will align with the qualitative case study principles that Yin (2014) advocated. Before and after the launching and implementation of interviews, surveys, and questionnaires, the researcher will ensure that questionnaires and interview questions are correctly written, interviewees' contact database is verified, interview tools-hardware and software-are functioning, calibrated, and working perfectly.

The study will also establish rapport with interviewees, read the introductory research script to the participants and inform or remind them that the interview will take not more than 35 minutes. Whether the interview is conducted online or onsite, the study will ensure that they have received and signed the Informed Consent Form and ask if there are any questions before beginning the primary interview. Moreover, prior to engaging participants in the interview, IRB approval will be requested, and a copy of the research protocol, including the interview guide, will be made available to participants. The interview protocol will proceed sequentially. The interviewer with commence asking small questions and then proceed to larger or complicated questions. The focus is to obtain evidence from each answer that the interviewee attempts to provide (Yin, 2014).

As Yin (2014) indicated, it is good to listen attentively and not interrupt interviewees when they are commenting or responding to questions. Participants' perceptions and views about PM phenomena emanate from deep reflection and introspection. Interrupting the flow of reflection may stymie their ability to provide detailed accounts of phenomena. Yin (2014) also encouraged researchers to accord participants courtesy and respect and request them to email or phone any additional data or information they may wish to provide after the interview. Expressing gratitude to participants or interviewees for their time and participation in the study and keeping track of the allotted time for the interview will also be religiously observed.

The questionnaires will contain 14 questions. These questions will consistently be aligned with the research questions, the research propositions, and the literature reviews. Generally, the proposed questionnaire includes the following: The participants will be asked to explain how the escalation of projectification, programmification, and globalization efforts have impacted their organization. How does PPGE expand the tasks and functions of projects or organizations? Do they believe the current project management theory thoroughly explains, describes, and predicts failure and success? How have these changes (due to PPGE) in managing projects affected the implementation of projects? In their experience, do these changes make it easier or harder to achieve business or project objectives? How do they think that knowledge of PM realities (due to PPGE efforts) can help manage projects or project-based organizations? How does the current project management theory underpin project practitioners or organizations to understand and predict the project's failure and success? Do PM practitioners think the current PM theory can fully explain, describe, and predict the project management domain due to PPGE efforts? How do they think the existing PM theory does not fully describe project management phenomena due to PPGE efforts? How have the current PM theoretical supports helped their organizations translate PM theory into practice? Do they think PM theory is essential to practitioners considering the high rate of project failure? How does a theory guide PM practitioners to reduce or increase the chances of project success or failure? Has the current theory's alleged failure to fully describe PM phenomena due to PPGE made developing a new theory necessary? How do they think having a full understanding or knowledge of the PPGE before undertaking a project increases the chances of managing or completing projects on time? (see Appendix E).

A pilot case study will be launched to test and validate these questions, equipment, and the research protocol's application encompassing procedures, methods, and ethics (Yin, 2009, 2014). The pilot is also an opportunity to practice and perfect the interview process with friends and associates. Participants' permission will be required prior to the official commencement of online and onsite surveys, interviews, and any other contact with participants. Surveys and interview questions will mostly be based on open-ended questions and the following themes: introduction, questions about expanding projects, programs, and global stakeholders, the impact of project, program and global effects on project management success, PM theoretical support, knowledge of the functions and tasks that practitioners perform, translating project management theory into practice, the importance of theory to project management practitioners, relationship between a theoretical understanding of project management phenomena and the increasing rate of project failure and the closing.

The study will ensure data collectors are qualified, and each category of a participant will receive the exact design instruments and is treated similarly. The involvement of multiple agents, including SurveyMonkey.com, Facebook survey, and Google Survey, attempts to reduce bias found in using a single data collector. Third-party agents recruited or hired to partake in the data collection and analysis will be trained and obliged to observe research protocols (Hsu and Sandford, 2012). The study's data collection will also include interview recording, transcription, coding, and analysis.

Interview Recording

Studies show that an interview is quintessential to the conduct of case study research. It facilitates the expression of participants' profound feelings about phenomena. The study will use Olympus WS-852 hardware to record interviews. This handheld digital recorder can record up to 1600 hours of audio and can compress data in mp3 file format. It is also USB ported. This makes it easy to manage data, transfer or import data to personal computers, and qualitative research data analysis software applications such as ATLAS.ti for transcriptions. Interviewees will be informed that the interview will be recorded and that they hold the right to refuse or accept the recording. They will further be asked to indicate whether they have fully understood the questions even though absolute data security is hard to guarantee, especially data collected through scraping on web-assisted sites. The study will ensure data encryption and storage in a secure Dropbox-cloud computing location or server through a well-thought-out data security plan. Only authorized personnel will have access.

Transcription

To convert recorded audio and video file to quality written format, the transcription strategy will be achieved in two fashions, namely, to hire a transcription service and use a Computer Assisted Qualitative Data Analysis Software (CAQDAS) including ATLAS. ti.8. Both have viable transcription and mp3 file import features (Friese, 2014). Transcription software services such as www.rev.com and transcript.com possess state-of-the-art technologies capable of transcribing video and audio files accurately and at competitive prices. If the researchers encounter PM practitioners or proxies who may not speak English as a primary language, the study will engage the services of www.transcriptionpanda.com. It has a proven record of transcribing foreign language audio and video files into English with accuracy. The application of ATLAS.ti 8 makes the importation of audio and video files seamless (Friese, 2014; Miles et al., 2014). They also enable watching video or listening to audio files while transcribing their contents. The researcher will sign a Confidentiality Agreement with the service providers to engage any outside services such as translation and transcription. The purpose of such nondisclosure agreements will focus on protecting the research data, especially the identity of participants, from harm.

Coding Management

highlight a direct quote from a participants' response, create a code, describe it, and give it an operational definition. The use of the query tool makes it quicker to populate cases that share similarities, and they can all be linked together. The application can also integrate video, text, and audio files. This symmetric mapping of coded concepts and quotes will be essential to the research in two ways. First, it makes the application easily de-identify a participant's personal information. Second, it identifies whether the link among participants' responses to survey or interview questions is assoc

Through Atlas-ti 8, the researcher can iated with, part of, cause of, contradictory to, or property of the phenomena that is being investigated. A word cruncher tool can also sort the frequently used words in survey responses. In other words, the ATLAS.ti 8 application enables the use of letters, numbers, and symbols to create code. This makes it easier to query a group of associated or related codes alphabetically (Friese, 2014; Miles et al., 2014). The application can also use concepts to represent a group of related cases or units such as construction, transportation, health care, IT, pharmaceutics, education, and management. Another essential feature of the ATLAS. ti8 in coding is its supercoding feature used to create other codes seamlessly.

Analysis

The analysis phase consists of organizing, tabulating, categorizing, identifying common or dissimilar patterns, and coding data. It also examines, questions data, and resolves any bias's appearance, the existence of which may cast doubt or aspersion on the validity and trustworthiness of the data. The research study to achieve success in analyzing data will implement two strategic policies: to use the seven theoretical propositions and a checklist to guide the process. The study will ensure that the literature review, the research questions, and the survey questions remain inextricably linked to the propositions (see Appendix G). The checklist will prioritize specific areas quintessential to the success of the research. It will also ensure that nothing is inadvertently missed or ignored. An excellent quality data analysis process will also require treating raw data, transcription, and interpretations keenly, analytically, and methodically (Yin, 2014).

The researcher will gather data mainly from two equivalent sources: PPGE-based organizations or case units and PM practitioners from PMI chapter members. There will be seven industries and eight units selected from each of the PPG-based organizations. Equally, there will be eight PM participants selected from PMI chapters in seven geographic locations worldwide. The study will compare dissimilarities between PM current theory and Project management theory 2.0 by analyzing data, events, and codes with codes (Sbaraini et al., 2011).

Computer-Aided Qualitative Data Analysis Software (CAQDAS) such as ATLAS.ti will be used to manage the analysis and coding of data. ATLAS.ti 8 version provides flexibility in creating code prefixes such as letters, metonymies, numbers, or symbols. For instance, the following codes viz. Con-case-1, Edu-case-1, HHs-case-1, IT-case-1, Mgmt-case-1, Phar-case -1, and Tran-case-1 have been created to represent the seven PPG-based industries, including construction, education, health care, information technology, management, pharmaceutical, and transportation. Con-case-1 represents the first unit of analysis within the construction industry. If the concept, construction, is used as a family code and a shortcut, it will group all construction case study codes such as con-case-1, con-case-2, con-case-3, con-case-4...con-case-8. The researcher may create a group of codes together, such as Edu-case-1, Edu-case-2, Edu-case-1edu-case-1, under the concept, education. The groping of family codes makes it easier to manage multiple codes concurrently and instantly. They also help to compare codes across various case studies and sites. ATLAS.ti also makes it seamless for a qualitative researcher to highlight notes, memos, transcribed texts, click on the Codes tab, create a code or a quote, and give it a name.

Primary document file format includes Microsoft Word, Rich Text Format (RTF), Portable Document Format (PDF), and Excel. Graphic file formats that the software can handle consist of Joint Photographic Experts Group (JPEG), Portable Network Graphics (PNG), and Graphics Interchange Format (GIF). Moving Picture Experts Group (MPEG), Windows Media Video (WMV), Audio-Video Interleaved (AVI), MP4, and Waveform Audio File Format (WAV) are some of the multimedia file formats that ATLAS.ti 8 can employ ("ATLAS.ti," 2012). In other words, ATLAS.ti 8 application enables the researcher to highlight quotes from interview transcripts and code them. This makes comparing, contrasting, and grouping together similar or dissimilar data coherent and accurate.

Assumptions

Exploring the development of a new PM theory assumes that the philosophical and methodological choice and the research design and implementation will logically work in tandem to achieve the research purpose. The multiple case study method assumes that participants, including PM practitioners and the case study units of analysis or their proxies, will have the knowledge, experience, and unobstructed cooperation to deeply explain their points of view and perspectives regarding the impact of PPGE on the PM domain. The application of the quantitative methodology in developing PM theory is widespread. However, its deterministic and narrow perspective of phenomena is not broad enough to comprehensively explain the PM domain due to PPGE efforts (Reksoatmodjo et al., 2012).

The study assumes that the research-designed instruments such as interview, survey, and archival will generate accurate and unblemished data. It also assumes that the design instruments will not favor or bias one respondent over another and that all of them will be asked the same questions and treated alike. Further, it is anticipated that whoever shall be asked to assist in the research's conduct and execution will be qualified and in compliance with all aspects of established protocols. The research investigators will exhibit a sense of professionalism, courtesy, and quality in the research process. Further, the study assumes that data will be gathered and managed according to the ethics and requirements that the qualitative case study method and the scientific community have ascribed. Participants will understand the interview or survey questions and respond to them accurately, thoroughly, and honestly.

Limitations

A multiple case study method limits the research to seek answers to the how what and why questions, excluding questions of quantitative nature. The lack of cause-and-effect relationship among case study constructs has led many experts to presume that qualitative research results are susceptible to subjectivity (Baxter and Jack, 2008; Jackson, 2012). Moreover, unlike single case research that usually describes a case unit of analysis in detail and is often parsimonious, multiple case study is limited to providing detailed analyses of case study units of analysis (Eisenhardt and Graibner, 2007; Yin, 2003). Identifying disparate and common patterns across case study units of analysis across multiple sites facilitates the evaluation of a theory development based on criteria such as credibility, transferability, dependability, reliability, and confirmability (De Massis and Kotlar, 2014; Yin, 2014).

Delimitations

The delimitations imposed on the research are intended to achieve specific strategic goals, such as selecting organizations and participants with the experience and knowledge of the impact of PPGE on the PM domain. This will make it easier for participating units and PM practitioners to provide in-depth explanations of PM phenomena' points of view. In other words, the design and conduct of multiple case studies focus exclusively on PPGE-based organizations and PMI chapter-based member practitioners. This excludes traditional single PM organizations and delimits the population and sample size to 112 in total, 56 selected from PPG-based organizations and 56 PMI chapter members and PM practitioners. In addition, the purposive selection of seven industries consisting of construction, transportation, health care, IT, pharmaceutical, education, and management out of which the units of analysis will emanate also demarcates the scope of the research (Eriksson and Kovalainen, 2012).

Ethical Assurances

This study will not do human, animal, and drug testing experiments; surveys, interviews, and sampling require contact and interaction with participants. Studies show that unregulated and unethical research can lead to physical harm, psychological stress, invasion of privacy, deception, coercion, or death (Committee on Science, Engineering, and Public Policy, 2009). The research will guarantee permission, respect, autonomy, safety, just treatment, and participants' protection. The Internal Review Board's approval will be requested before the raw data gathering process's commencement. The studies' results will also be presented accurately and avoid misconduct, deception, lack of commitment, confounding variables, and biases. It will also ensure that the survey samples are worded, and the study goal is fully achieved (Bennett et al., 2014). Besides, the research will perform the following ethical goals: (a) protection from harm, (b) informed consent, (c) right to privacy, (d) honesty with professional colleagues, (e) parental assent, and (f) beneficence (g).

Protection from Harm

The research will control behaviors and actions that could compromise the Hippocratic Oath to not harm stakeholders, in general, and particularly to participants (American Psychological Association [APA], 2010; Koocher, 2014).

Informed consent

In consonance with the Belmont Report, the research will inform and seek participants' consent before the raw data gathering process begins. The research investigators will explain to participants about the research objective, its risks, and benefits and how research investigators will maintain data integrity (Aggarmal and Gurnani, 2014; Aggarmal and Gurnani, 2014).

Prior to officially scheduling an interview with potential human participants, the study will obtain a full consent agreement with each participant. The study will liaise with their legal representatives to do so for those who are disabled or illiterate and unable to sign the consent form. Participants will also have full access to a list of contacts that they can call or email if they have cold feet, want to withdraw from the research, or simply intend to seek additional information.

Right to Privacy

The study will protect participants' right to privacy, confidentiality, and self-determination irrespective of their socioeconomic status.

Honesty with Professional Colleagues

The honest and just treatment of participants, including investigators, assistants, moral, financial supporters, communities, and the world at large, will be of paramount importance to the research.

Parental Assent

Establish a signed Parental Consent Agreement form with parents and will be required if the research intends to recruit children to participate in the study.

Beneficence

Before participants are engaged in the study, they will be informed about the benefit and reward that the research intends to do for them (Hirshon et al., 2013). The outcome of a good and ethical investigation can benefit everyone. This research will value those who contribute to solving problems related to project management theory.

Summary

The research method reflects the research problem statement, purpose, questions, multiple case study design, and implementation procedure. It also addresses the assumptions, limitations, delimitations, and ethical assurance considerations. PPGE has increased the PM domain. This is evident by the integration of PM's temporary functions and operations of permanent organizations. The marked absence of PM's existing theory to fully explain and predict PM phenomena' success and failure has created an ontological and epistemological fissure. PMT 2.0 is being proposed to fill that gap. How does PPGE impact PM theoretical foundations, and to what extent does developing a new theory undergird PM practitioners to optimize PM success?

The research investigators will use a multiple case study method to achieve the purpose of this dissertation research. Its strengths include using multiple research design instruments such as surveys, interviews, and archival documentation to gather data from participants across multiple locations. SurveyMonkey.com, Facebook survey, and Google Survey application will facilitate reaching targeted participants. The raw data sources will stem from participants' feelings and experiences that they will express (McKusker and Gunaydin, 2015). Critics say that a case study method is generally susceptible to reliability and generalizability problems (Yin, 2014). A total of 112 participants will be purposively selected from PPGE based organizations (N =56) and PMI chapter members (N =56) across multiple geographic sites.

The study procedure will consist of planning the research, selecting the cases, designing the study protocol, collecting the data, analyzing, and interpreting the data, and reporting the findings (De Massis and Kotlar, 2014; Yin, 2014). The study assumes that the research questions, propositions, method, research instruments, and protocol will produce credible, transferable, dependable, reliable, and confirmable results. The study is limited to a qualitative line of questioning of who, what, and why (Baxter and Jack, 2008; Jackson, 2012). The research is delimited by choice of participants whose experience and knowledge will provide empirical evidence needed to either confirm or disconfirm the emergent theory. The study will comply with standards that Northcentral University (NCU), Institutional Review Board (IRB), and the conduct of multiple case study methods have ascribed, sanctioned, and encouraged.

CHAPTER 4

Findings

Overview

The purpose of the research study was twofold: to develop a new project management theory and to provide PM practitioners a broader understanding of the impact of projectification, program-mification, and globalization escalation (PPGE) on the PM field of study. It also compared the extant PM theory and the emergent theory, aka PMT2.0. The study was designed based on a multiple-case research study. Santos and Eisenhardt (2004) and Yin (2004, 2013, 2014) indicated multiple case studies were a better method in theory development, confirming or disconfirming an emerging theory. This makes the results obtained from applying multiple-case study research robust and generalizable. Put differently, the multiple case study enables researchers to gather data from a wide variety of sources, including open-ended survey questionnaires, observation, seminal works, peer review articles, and archival documents.

The research study selected 112 participants from the construction, health care, information technology, education, management, pharmaceutics, and transportation industries. Marshall et al. (2013) and Van Rijnsoever (2017) indicated that despite its cost and difficulty in collecting, organizing, analyzing, and coding a high volume of interview data, a large sample size provides a better simulation of the diversity of the sampling population. It also increases the likelihood of discovering contemporary theory and offers valuable and rigorous results.

About 1268 participants were asked to complete the research open-ended survey questionnaire. Two hundred and thirty-four consented to participate, and 156 of them completed the full interview. Forty-four were excluded when the study reached theoretical saturation. Theoretical saturation is achieved when the researcher is explicitly confident that the data collected are interconnected, thickly described the themes or categories, and the emergence of a new theory is feasible (Packer, 2011; Van Rijnsoever, 2017).

There were seven open-ended questions, and an average of two additional probed questions was asked drawn from each research question. For financial reasons, the in-person or direct phone interview was designed to be held only in the North American region. About 98.7 percent of participants chose the open-ended online survey questionnaire. The online survey questionnaires were designed to make autonomous participation, withdrawal, and disqualification of ineligible participants easier, including deleting incomplete responses and browsing through the databases for any data entry errors.

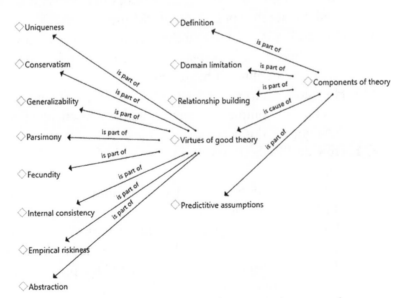

Figure 2. Criteria used to test and compare the extant theory and the emergent theory aka PMT2.0. The test results were compared to empirical evidence and literature review.

The online survey was also instrumental in preserving the quality of participants' responses from transcription errors and protecting the confidentiality of the data and participant contact information from third-party access. Responses were also protected from the potential interviewer's subtle or obvious bias and sway or insinuation. ATLAS.ti 8 software was used to create quotes, themes, categories, and qualitative network diagrams. Each research proposition and question were intended to ask the how and why types of questions about PPGE expansion of the PM domain. The research propositions helped focus the research on achieving its objective. Due to the controversiality of theory's nature and meaning, the study used the four essential elements of theory and the eight virtues of good theory criteria to measure PM theory and compare differences between the extant theory and the emergent theory (see Figure 2).

The search for empirical evidence for the research study was based on the following research questions:

Q1. How do PPGE efforts broaden the scope of the PM domain and impact the application of PM theory?

Q2. How do PPGE efforts limit the current PM theory's capacity to fully describe, explain, and predict complex, uncertain, and nonlinear phenomena?

Q3. How do a complete understanding, description, and prediction of complex, uncertain, and nonlinear phenomena impact a project's success?

Q4. How do PPGE efforts transform the PM domain and its theory?

Q5. How do these transformational efforts impact or influence PM theory and practice?

Q6. How does the development of a new PM theory (the proposed PMT2.0, for example) eliminate the gap between PM extant theory and the expansion of the project management domain due to PPGE?

Q7. What challenges have PM practitioners experienced due to PPGE efforts?

Chapter 4 contains a discussion on the research findings, the trustworthiness of data, study results, evaluation of findings, and is followed by the summary.

Trustworthiness of Data

Regarding research data collection, analysis, interpretation, and reporting, trustworthiness can be stymied by two interrelated factors. First, most researchers use a positivist methodology that generates data that do not truly represent participants' feelings or points of view. Second, researchers can become uncommitted to implementing research protocol and procedures. Standing alone or combining the two, these factors typically create questionable links between the research and a trustworthy outcome. Research protocols methodically guide the researcher to accurately observe, evaluate and analyze data that make sense in the real world (Gilbert, Ruigrok, and Wicki, 2008). The study was committed to the trustworthiness of the empirical data. It religiously followed research protocols, procedures, good practices, and standards that Northcentral University (NCU), Institutional Review Board (IRB), and the scientific research community have found not only acceptable but mandatory.

A multiple-case study design was appropriate for the study; it helped the researcher focus on gathering data and comparing those data from disparate units located in various sites (Yin, 2009, 2014). It also allowed the study to collect data from peer-review articles, archival records, interviews, open-ended survey questionnaires, and direct and indirect participant observation.

Moreover, according to Harlow (2010) and Yin (2009, 2014), a case study enables even the neophyte or fledgling researcher to develop a sound and virtuous theory through sufficient research design, theoretical propositions, and empirical data. The application of open-ended questionnaires, for instance, enabled Wendy Holloway and Tony Jefferson to gather empirical data and develop a new theory antithetical to the one that the British Crime Survey

(BSC) held on Gender difference, anxiety, and fear of crime. BSC gathered its data quantitively. Through the constructivist and interpretative research process, participants told their stories and points of view of realities freely and unobstructedly. These unobstructed responses helped Holloway and Jefferson understand that crime and anxiety's meanings impact people differently irrespective of gender difference. The emergence of new ideas obtained through interviews helped Holloway and Jefferson tested and developed a new theory that provides a body of knowledge on the fear of crime and anxiety in the United Kingdom. Their research results were also an eye-opener to researchers and policymakers worldwide (Harlow, 2010; Holloway and Jefferson, 2000).

Scholars and theorists agree that multiple case study methodology is appropriate for theory generating, development, and testing (Harlow, 2010; Yin, 2014). It empowers researchers to search the truth from diverse sources, observe reality from different perspectives, and ask open-ended questions that make the generation of participant points of view, idiosyncrasies, and feelings about PM phenomena feasible. The open-ended question survey encouraged participants to unearth what takes place in their natural and respective organizational milieus. Triangulation enhances the credibility of the research findings and reduces the likelihood of errors (Parylo, 2012); it complements, strengthens, and offsets weaknesses in each method. The research study endeavored to meet credibility, transferability, dependability, reliability, and confirmability criteria.

Credibility

The study used multiple design instruments, open-ended interview questions, surveys, archival documents, and peer review literature to gather evidence for the research. Before launching interviews, surveys, and questionnaires, the researcher verified interviewees' contact database and interview tools, including hardware and software, were functioning, calibrated, and worked flawlessly.

The research purposely selected participants from PM practitioners and chapters worldwide who had worked in the construction, education, health care, information technology, management, pharma, or transport industry (see Appendix N). Participants were not eligible if they were not 24 or older, college graduates, had not acquired a minimum of six months of experience managing aspects of projects, programs, or global-based organizations, and not fluent in reading and writing English. Potential participants were not selected based on gender preference; instead, they were targeted because their experience and knowledge about project management (PM) phenomena provided empirical evidence to confirm or disconfirm the emergent theory or the extant theory. Partially eligible participants, notably those who offered incomplete answers, did not read, understand, and sign the Consent Form, were excluded from the study.

The study used the following questions to screen prospective participants: Are you a project management practitioner? Are you a chapter member of the Project management Institute (PMI) or any of its affiliated project management organizations? Are you a college graduate? Have you worked in one of the following industries: construction, health care, information technology, management, pharmaceutics, or transportation? Are you at least 24 years old? Have you acquired over six months of experience managing aspects of project-based, program-based, or global-based organizations? Are you fluent in reading and writing English?

Transferability

Responses of the research participants were analogous and duplicatable. The upshoot of PPGE, namely project complexity, chaos, uncertainty, and nonlinearity, most notably impacted the construction health care, information technology, education, management, pharmaceutics, and transportation sectors than most other PM sectors. The knowledge of these complexities is consequently essential and replicable to managing complex projects in all industries.

The majority of participants from the seven major PM industries confirmed the study's propositions. For instance, the overwhelming participants, who had worked in these industries and served in managerial capacities, agreed that due to PPGE efforts, the PM domain has become complex, multifaceted, and harder to manage undertakings. Consequently, they noted that PM theory was becoming increasingly incapable of describing, explaining, and predicting multifaceted and complex phenomena; PPGE expansion integrates continuous organizational operations and PM finite functions, making it onerous to achieve sustainable success. They also agreed that a new theory is needed to describe, explain, and predict the behaviors of PPGE constructs and that complete understanding and knowledge of PPGE constructs were the sine qua non and a game changer from mortality (failure) to immortality (sustainable success) (Venkatesh, Brown, and Bala, 2013; Yilmaz, 2013).

Dependability

Knowledge of PM practice, its conceptualizations, especially the effects of PPGE on the current PM domain, was the primary criterion for purposively recruiting PM practitioners and PMI members and affiliated organizations. The open-ended survey questionnaire enabled the research to obtain practitioner's practical, theoretical, and in-depth points of view across multiple industries relevant to a complete understanding of the impact of PPGE on PM phenomena. Quotidianly, practitioners plan, execute, and monitor PPGE-based projects and implicitly or explicitly make significant decisions that affect PM's success and failures. In other words, PM practitioners provided substantial practical and theoretical information needed to fully understand the nuances of the impact of PPGE efforts on the current PM theory and compare PM current theory and the emergent PMT2.0. Literature confirmed that research participants could be motivated to provide high-quality and dependable data when participants are highly educated and experienced (see Appendix H).

Confirmability

The study applied case study methodology, literature review, and propositions to make confirmation and disconfirmation easier and transparent. Harlow (2009) and Stam (2000, 2006, 2010) acknowledged the significance of case studies in contributing to theory development. They explained that a case study could disprove an existing theory's viability and potentially contribute to theory building through empirical evidence and testing. Studies show that theory development and testing are interconnected (Harlow, 2010).

A researcher can retest a theory when a new set of data determine that the latest discovery is significant enough to replace the existing theory through retroduction. Harlow (2009, 2010) stated that the process of theory development is recursive or cyclical: the researcher can gather data through observations, surveys, interviews, or case studies to test an extant theory. If the data fail to validate the theory, the researcher can reject the research results and move on or start an entirely new project. However, if the data provide sufficient empirical evidence to invalidate the current theory, a new theory is espoused.

Wacker (1998) identified four basic theoretical criteria viz., conceptual definition, domain limitations, relationship-building, and prediction. Van de Ven (1989) indicated that theory spurs knowledge, enlightenment, and undergirds professionals' organizational management activities. Gelso (2006) and Wacker (1998) also distinguished a soi-disant theory from a virtuous one on the following criteria: uniqueness, parsimony, conservatism, generalizability, fecundity, internal consistency, empirical riskiness, and abstraction (see Figure 2).

Whetten (1989) noted that for a theory to be considered complete, it must respond to the following factors: what, how, why, who, where, and when. To confirm or disconfirm any scientific theory requires testing the emergent theory or the current theory to see if each meets the basic and essential theoretical elements and the criteria of virtues of a good theory. The control chart explains the steps required to do this effectively (see Appendix L).

The study used eight propositions to narrow the research's focus and test if each research question is linked to the research study's purpose (see Table 8). Sufficient condition, a necessary condition, and deterministic relation are critical proportional concepts used in developing and evaluating PMT 2.0 (Dul and Hak, 2008). These evaluation concepts contribute to either verifying an old assumption or testing a new one about PM phenomena.

Conceptually, a sufficient condition exists when a specific value of concept A results in a particular value of concept B. For instance, when the PM current theory meets a1, a2, a3, a4 values, PM theory will fully explain, describe, and predict PM phenomena. In other words, if PM theory meets the criteria of the basic essential components of theory and those of virtues and good theory, it can thoroughly explain and predict PPGE complex, nonlinear, and uncertain phenomena. Besides, when only the PM current theory fulfills a1, a2, a3, a4 requirements, it will be comparatively superior to the emergent theory.

A necessary condition exists if a specific value of concept B exists if there is a particular value of concept A. For instance, PMT2.0 is only comparably superior if it fulfills the criteria of the essential four theoretical elements and the eight virtues of a good theory. Deterministic relation exists when an increase in concept A consistently results in a change (in a consistent direction) in the value of concept B. If a genuine theory exists because it meets the good and virtuous criteria, there cannot be a good or genuine theory without fully meeting these criteria. If A (good and virtuous criteria) is required for B, then B cannot exist or be considered genuine without meeting the characteristics of a good and virtuous theory. Virtues of a good theory are necessary and sufficient conditions for any genuine or scientific theory (Dul and Hak, 2008).

Each proposition in this study was tested using necessary and sufficient conditional relations criteria (see Table 8). If the observed value is different from the actual value, the proposition is said to be false. If, on the other hand, the observed value matches the real value, the proposition is considered truthful. In case the proposition is accurate, the study can replicate the results.

Results

The research recruited PM experts to provide in-depth views regarding the impact of PPGE on the PM domain and the necessity of developing a new theory. In the research questions and propositions, the research study frequently used the terms *transform, predict PM phenomena, complexity, theory, nonlinear, PPGE constructs, broaden the scope, impact the application,* and *the capacity to explain.* The terms were either a part of or explained the vital elements of a good theory's theory and virtues. Participants were asked to share their views and experiences about the impact of these terms on PM theory and the industry or environment where they worked or lived.

Three themes emerged from participants' responses, including cited works and the research propositions. These themes were grouped into three slots: existing theoretical, predictive, or emergent theoretical outcomes, and theoretical benefits of the emergent theory (see Figure 3). The existing theoretical situation described how PPGE expansion enlarged the PM domain and limited its theory to explain complex phenomena fully. Participants believed that the lack of full understanding and knowledge of PPGE constructs contributed to the high rate of PPGE-based project mortality. Questions asked to solicit participants' responses in the first slot were Q1, Q2, Q4, and Q5.

In the second predictive or emergent theoretical outcomes slot, the research study asked participants how the knowledge gap between PPGE expansion efforts and PM theory could be resolved. The questions asked were Q3 and Q6. Participants believed that knowledge of PPGE constructs was a game changer between project mortality and immortality.

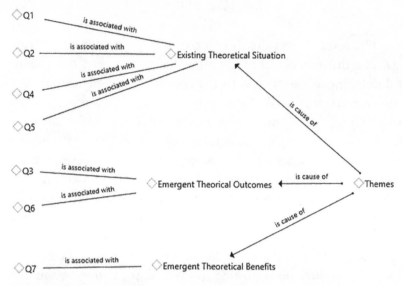

Figure 3. The three thematic slots along with corresponding questions.

They agreed that a new theory that would link PPGE constructs to PM practical realities logically was needed. In the last slot, the theoretical benefits of the emergent theory, the study asked participants Q7. Their responses showed that the emergent theory should have the ability to describe, explain, and predict PPGE constructs effectively. Significant benefits included providing participants the theoretical underpinnings so that they can be able to understand the complexity of PPGE phenomena fully. They believed a theory aligned with the PPGE phenomena could help them effectively translate theory into practice.

A total of 112 participants was purposely selected to participate in the research study. There were (N = 56) chosen from major PPGE-based organizations consisting of construction, health care, education, IT, management, pharmaceutical, and transportation. Equally, PM practitioners (N = 56) were recruited from various PMI chapter-based geographic regions. Geographically, 19 from Europe completed the online open-ended survey questionnaire, nine from the Middle East, 61 from North America, nine from Asia, five from Africa, and nine from South America. Eighteen participants came from construction, 21 from education, nine from health care, 33 from IT, 40 from management, four from pharmaceutics, and five from transportation. The population sample's geographic dispersion increased the generalizability of the research (see Appendix H).

Existing Theoretical Situation

Research Question 1. How do PPGE efforts broaden the scope of the PM domain and impact the application of PM theory?

Question 1. How do PPGE efforts broaden the scope of the PM domain and impact the application of PM theory?

Proposition 1. If a good and virtuous theory provides a full description, definition, explanation, and prediction of phenomena, then PM theoretical boundary will expand due to PPGE efforts.

In the first thematic category, about 31 percent of respondents indicated that PPGE efforts expanded the PM domain's scope through finite function and continuous organizational operations integration. Some participants explained the PPGE expansion of the PM domain, the impact on PM theory, and how to deal with it:

> "[My organization/company/business] deals with short-time activities while projectification, programmification, and globalization require long-term commitments. They [PPGE efforts] mean a more standard organizational structure with processes devoted to increased business success and risk in project management, program management, and international endeavors. We will need more funding and adaptability to meet the ever-increasing challenges and uncertainties that these terms impact organizations."

Table 1
Q1: PPGE Expansion Efforts

Themes	Frequency	%
Integrate finite and permanent business functions	35	31
Deal with disparate socioeconomic and legal systems	25	22
Expand opportunities and risks across frontiers	15	13
Handle global stakeholders' pressures	14	13
Confront multiple resistant factors across frontiers	16	14
PPGE efforts have no impact	7	6

Note: N = 112

This question was posed against the following proposition that asserted that if a good and virtuous theory provides a full description, definition, explanation, and prediction of phenomena, then PM's theoretical boundary will expand due to PPGE efforts. In other words, the who and what defines the anatomy of the theory-the ontological elements-that outline the conceptual and theoretical constructs (Gelso, 2006). If those elements do not form an integral part of a theory, internal inconsistency and relationship problems will ensue among the constructs. This will weaken the theory's capacity to fully describe, explain and, more importantly, predict what could, should, and would occur if an organization intends to pursue strategy policy changes needed to achieve sustainable outcomes.

The combination of themes such as dealing with disparate socioeconomic and legal systems, expanding opportunities and risks across frontiers, handling global stakeholders' pressures, and confronting multiple resistant factors across boundaries were the consequence of PPGE expansion efforts. As far as PPGE efforts have no impact, only 6 percent of respondents agreed. The seven respondents put it this way:

> "I don't believe it [PPGE] directly affected my project. We do projects and programs, but there's not a structured/formal approach. Our organization outsources project and program management. They overburnt our internal team with functions and tasks. I never heard those terms. Don't affect my organization."

In addition, Project-based organizations (PBOs) integrate an enterprise's management tasks and manage the relationships between project units and their internal and external environments (Kwak et al., 2015). Muller et al. (2016) added that PBOs centralize PM activities within the enterprise and balance PM functionalities and the enterprise's strategic responsibilities. Globalization expands the market horizons, drives innovation, toughens the competition, and increases stakeholders' engagement and interdependencies across borders (Bodislav et al., 2015; Vongprasuth and Choi, 2014).

PMT 2.0 theoretical foundation recognized, as most respondents indicated, PM domain had been expanded due to PPGE efforts. Thus, organizations paradoxically perform multiple roles and functions without fully understanding the complexity of those constructs' makeup. This has reduced organizations' ability to predict, with accuracy, constructs' behaviors and what policy they can implement to sustain a competitive edge. PMT2.0 provides the answers to the who, what, when, where, how, why, could, should, and would questions. It is evaluated against the criteria and virtues of a good theory. PM 2.0's propositions are also tested by sufficient conditions, necessary conditions, deterministic relations, and probabilistic relations.

Research

Question 2. How do PPGE efforts limit the current PM theory's capacity to fully describe, explain, and predict complex, uncertain, and nonlinear phenomena?

Proposition 2. Practitioners will not fully achieve success until PM theory can explain and predict PPGE constructs.

Generally, a high number of participants thought PPGE had expanded the PM domain and, per consequence, entangled its theoretical effectiveness (See Table 2). A decade ago, PMI predicted the creation of over 15.7 million new PM jobs. In 2013 another prediction was made that in 2016, 1.2 million PM jobs were created in various sectors (Project Management Institute [PMI], 2013).

Table 2
Q2: PPGE Expansion Impact

Theme	Frequency	%
Broadens PM theoretical boundary	30	27
Creates complex and uncertain structures	28	25
It makes it harder to undergird practitioners	16	14
Weakens PM current theory	33	29
It makes no difference	5	4

Note. N = 112

Recipients of project management certifications are over 600,000 in the US alone (Lundqvist and Marcusson, 2014). Among the 112 volunteers who participated in the research study, about 98.7 percent were PMP certified. Besides the seven industries where they were purposively recruited, about 88 percent had managed projects in other sectors. These include manufacturing, financial, mining, banking, Federal Govt., consultancy, energy, engineering, environmental, telecommunication, audio-visual, and non-profit organizations.

Irrespective of a shift toward Agile and Prince 2 methodologies, to name a few, PM theory remains limited to the effects of PPGE phenomena. While these expansion and convergent efforts had augmented the complexity, nonlinearity, uncertainty, and chaos of PM, PM's extant theory has not kept pace with the dictates of these emergent, evolutionary, and intricate neologisms. Most participants explained the limited capacity of the current PM theory to fully describe, explain, and predict complex, uncertain, and nonlinear phenomena in the following manner:

> "The PM domain expansion increases the complexity and application of tools and techniques amongst project practitioners and their teams. This reduces the chance of completing projects on time. The more you expand, the more unwieldy PM theory becomes a predictor of project success. The current theory does not measure a project team's ability to *roll with the punches* and a project manager's ability and timing to know when to *punch back* while keeping the team focused. It seems there is an absence of PM theory capable of describing and predicting these complex realities."

A limited number of participants, about 5 percent, thought that PPGE expansion had no effects on the current PM theory:

> "[I, we] don't believe any project management plan can predict the success or failure of a project. Current PM theory has provided my organization, the theoretical support that is required, to predict the failure or success of a project."

Research Question 4. How do PPGE efforts transform the PM domain and its theory?

Proposition 4. Permanent and finite function integration create manifold uncertainties.

Oerlemans and Pretorius (2014) pointed out PPGE has pervaded sundry academic fields, including organizational sciences and inter-organizations, megaprojects, and joint ventures, to name a few. Moreover, because of PPGE, the project management field has shifted from a mere emphasis on a project's scope, time, and cost to apply a holistic approach to managing projects. Battistuzzo and Piscopo (2015) and Trkman (2010) explained that PPGE expands the endogenous and exogenous risks and challenges of international projects. The changes that PPGE brings about impact PM's domain significantly, making the field nonlinear and impervious to prescriptive, deterministic, and linear solutions.

Table 3

Question 4: Expansion of PM Theoretical Boundary

Theme	Frequency	%
Integrates local and global activities	34	30
It makes PPGE-based projects far-fetched	26	23
Creates complex working environments	25	22
Deals with multiple global stakeholders	15	13
Hard to measure PM theoretical impact	12	11

Note. N = 112

Rigby et al. (2014) explained that PPGE exacerbates PM policymaking gridlock, bureaucracy, and resistance. It is complex, arduous, and requires forethought and a deep understanding of the interconnectivity and dynamism among stakeholders across borders. The current prescriptive management approaches cannot predict the unpredictable unknowns in managing complex projects. This hiatus has added to the litany of PM pathologies. Approximately 60 percent of worldwide annual investment in projects fails (Flyvbjerg, 2014).

These transformative efforts have reverberated in motley management circles across industries and frontiers. About 30 percent of respondents confirmed that through PPGE efforts, local businesses are increasingly globalized and multifaceted (see Table 3). This, according to most respondents, had made PPGE-based projects far-fetched, created a complex working environment, multiplied stake-holders across frontiers, and made it challenging to measure PM theoretical impact.

"PPGE efforts deal with lots of complex and interconnected moving parts that are controlled and sponsored by stakeholders across many geographic regions. It is complex and uncertain; our products must comply with diverse international governing market bodies' standards. My current project involves resources from different countries. We have to coordinate with our Asian associates to gather requirements and work together to complete the project fully."

There was a pocket of those who thought, among other things, that:

> "The current processes require a new approach that is a combination of agile, scrum, PMBOK, and other approaches... Project management theoretical domain depends on the managers."

Research Question 5. How do these transformational efforts impact or influence PM theory and practice?

Proposition 5. These various uncertainties have impeded practitioners' efforts to achieve optimum success.

Godenhjelm et al. (2014), Lundin and Sjoblom (2014), and Rijke et al. (2014) stated that the effects of projectification, programmification, and globalization had transformed the PM domain, expanding its theoretical linchpin beyond its capacity to explain, describe, and predict these manifold realities fully. Godenhjelm et al. (2014) and Packendorf and Lindgren (2013) argued that PPGE increases a project's environmental, political, entrepreneurial constructs, and complexities changing traditional and prescriptive views of PM into strategic organizations that operate permanently.

Table 4
Q5: PM's Complexity, Chaos, Uncertainty, and Nonlinearity

Theme	Frequency	%
Slow project implementation	27	24
Make constructs harder to understand	30	27
Increase large-scale projects failures	16	14
Make PM practice difficult	15	13
Create manifold activities that impact the PM domain	18	16
There is no PPGE impact	6	5

Note. N = 112

The integration of PM temporaneous function and the perpetual operation of PPGE-based organizations have raised significant conceptual, contextual, and theoretical challenges for PM, as a distinct field of academic discipline including PM practitioners, but seems paradoxical. Godenhjelm et al. (2014) explained that PM's temporal existence and innovative capacity might be overshadowed or fragmented by the complex and monolithic structure that PPGE creates. In other words, the conflation of permanent and temporal functions presents a paradigm shift and a significant organizational and cultural change.

The fifth research proposition stated that if a theory meets the criteria of a good and a virtuous theory, as measured by the criteria drawn from Gelso (2006), Harlow (2009, 2010), and Wacker (1998), then a complete understanding of phenomena due to PPGE efforts will increase. And as a result, translating theory into practice will be more accurate and predictable. To be considered as virtues and good theoretical criteria, a theory must expand when its territorial domain increases due to events that significantly affect its modus operandi as well as its raison d'etre.

The four essential elements of theory (see Figure 2) function jointly. When the territorial boundary is not clear and specific, the definition becomes nebulous, and the theory will not be able to build relationships or connections among constructs or variables logically. In the absence of internal consistency, the theory will indeed become incapable of clearly and precisely explaining, describing, or predicting constructs' behaviors. There are no trade-offs in being considered a superior theory and not meeting the virtues of a good theory. The definition of theory is a necessary part of a theory but not sufficient for a theory to claim legitimacy. The presence of a clear territorial boundary, the ability to build logical relationships among constructs, and to explain and predict events using auxiliary verbs such as could, should, and would must also be considered (Dul and Hak, 2008)

Wacker (1998) agreed that for a theory to enjoy the scientific community's approbation and validity, it must clearly define phenomena, establish a defined domain and territorial limitations, create relationships among its constructs, and predict events among those constructs' variables. Wacker (1998, 2004)) further indicated that it must meet the criteria of virtues of a good theory for a theory to be noteworthy. Participants showed that PPGE expansion caused a slow project implementation and a high rate of large-scale project mortality. Most respondents, according to Table 5, echoed these sentiments thus:

> "[The impact of PPGE effects on PM theory or practice] provide global structures that are complex and hard to achieve. They [PPGE efforts] widen the focus, expose the paradox of integrating temporal and continuous PM functions, and understand PM activities' complexity and uncertainty. If the project management theory is not equally enlarged, it [PM domain] could implode."

Some respondents thought about the PPGE expansion efforts in this manner:

> "PPGE efforts are complex and novel, making it inherently impossible for practitioners of the current PM theory to control projects and pre-

dict outcomes. These efforts provide the basis for introspection to seek new templates, tools, and methodologies to complete complex projects."

5 percent, however, thought that PPGE expansion had altered nothing with regard to PM domain or their organizations:

"None of my employers used project management theory as a tool to predict project success or failure. Besides the PMBOK, I don't see any other impact. It's hard to tell whether PM theory guides or impacts any of the works we do."

Emergent Theoretical Outcomes

Research Question 3. How do a complete understanding, description, and prediction of complex, uncertain, and nonlinear phenomena impact a project's success?

Proposition 3. Complete knowledge of PPGE constructs changes PM mortality to immortality.

Table 5
Q3: Complete Knowledge of PPGE Constructs

Theme	Frequency	%
Changes failure to success	32	29
IT makes PPGE constructs understood	26	23
Provides support and guidance	27	24
Breeds creativity/ innovations	12	11
Provides consistency and predictability	15	13

Note. N = 112

The Advanced English Dictionary defines the theory and "an organized system of accepted knowledge that applies in various circumstances to explain a specific set of phenomena." Harlow (2009, 2010) explained that a theory provides order and understanding of phenomena. Lalonde et al. (2010) indicated that PM theory deepens practitioners' and researchers' understanding of epistemological issues in the field of project management. They suggested that an epistemological issue regarding PM theory could be practical (heuristic), quantitative, qualitative, and reflective (qualitative and pragmatic). A heuristic discipline is mainly concerned about PM's practical aspects like what practitioners do daily in managing projects. Understanding PM theory is therefore important to practitioners; it impacts projects' success. According to Table 5, about 99 percent of participants thought that understanding PM theory impacts PM success, makes PPGE constructs understood, provides support and guidance, breeds creativity/ innovations, provides consistency and predictability, and reduces failure of complex projects.

O'Brien (2017) indicated that an organization would not succeed without an in-depth and holistic understanding, description, and predictability of PPGE phenomena' behavior. The higher the competence or ability to deeply grok the effects of PPGE on the PM field of study, the sooner organizations will bounce from chaos, uncertainty, and mortality to immortality. In other words, managing complex, chaotic, and uncertain projects require a highly talented, skillful, and expert team. The higher the mastery and knowledge of the complex situation's nuance, the less complicated and more opportune it becomes (See Appendix H).

He et al. (2013) noted that lack of relevant knowledge about complex projects leads to dismal performance, cost overrun, and schedule delays. Yang et al. (2013) added that complex organizations characterized by project, program, and global undertakings require knowledge leadership or theory that promotes a profound understanding of organizational complex construct or customer management. This is what most participants thought about the significance of knowledge in the PM field:

"Yes, knowledge provides us a better understanding of projects, especially complex, global-based, project-based projects. Yes, success in managing a complex business or organization, or project depends on knowledge and understanding the uncertainties, weaknesses, and strengths. The project management depends on the principle of a professional's ability to finish the project."

Research Question 6. How does the development of a new PM theory (the proposed PMT 2.0, for example) eliminate the gap between PM extant theory and the expansion of the project management domain due to PPGE?

Proposition 6: A new theory, PMT2.0, is being developed to explain and predict the impact of PPGE.

PPGE has expanded PM extant theory domain beyond the iron triangle (Artto et al., 2015; Godenhjelm et al., 2014; Rijke et al., 2014). The expansion has also gone beyond the temporality and project lifecycle contextualization. This limited vista makes PM extant theory ineffective in predicting events that may drive complex organizations to succeed or fail. Artto et al. (2015), Godenhjelm et al. (2014), and Rijke et al. (2014), along with most of the research participants, indicated that a new theory was needed to describe, explain, and predict the behaviors of PPGE constructs.

PM's trilogy and temporality are no longer considered panaceas to PM ills (Oellgaard, 2013; Besteiro, Pinto, and Novaski, 2015), especially in the face of PPGE expansion efforts. PM trilogy tries to balance a project's scope, schedule, and cost (Besteiro et al., 2015; Oellgaard, 2013). The new theory's theoretical foundation, aka PMT2.0, must answer the who, what, when, where, how, why, could, should, and would question and resolve the gap between PPGE and the extant PM theory. PMT 2.0 also evaluates against the criteria and virtues of good theory (see Appendix L).

Table 6
Q6: The Emergent Theory

Theme	Frequency	%
Provides good and virtuous theoretical framework	41	37
Guides practitioner's efforts to predict phenomena	25	22
Expands PM landscape/environment	13	12
Serves as the basis for PM methodology	12	11
Guide for good PM practice	15	13
PMT 2.0 is not necessary	6	5

Note. N = 112

The new theory takes a holistic approach in achieving success by ensuring that there is an alignment between PPGE constructs and PM theoretical or philosophical foundation and that complete knowledge and understanding of PPGE constructs are catalysts to sustaining organizational competitiveness. PMT2.0 defines a project as temporary or permanent undertakings created to develop a product or provide a service to achieve a specific objective.

PMT2.0 measures PM success or failure and guides practitioners to understand PPGE semantics through three basic conceptualizations explained in a five-step process (see Appendix M). The elements of this tripartite conceptualization are as follows: projectification, programmification, and globalization escalation (PPGE), complex, chaotic, uncertain, and nonlinear phenomena (CCUNP), and mortality (failure)

PPGE is defined as the predictor, mortality, the outcome, and CUUNP, the mediator. CUUNP is related to or associated with PPGE and mortality. PPGE's expansion directly impacts mortality and indirectly elevates the CUUNP level of complexity. Stated differently, the mediator explains the extent to which the predictor (PPGE) influences or controls the outcome (mortality) (Karazsia, Berlin, Amstrong, Janicke, and Darling, 2013). If the mediating effects contradict what is observed, the mediator becomes ineffective. The replication of CUUNP across construction, transportation, information technology, health care, pharmaceutics, management, and education industries determine the strength of the association between CUUNP and PPGE (see Table 9).

PMT2.0 espouses the notion that knowledge mediates between sustainable success (immortality) and mortality. The higher the level of knowledge, training, and experience, the better the conversion from mortality to immortality. This accords with the overwhelming views of participants and research proposition four and proposition 7. Proposition 4. Stated that if knowledge is the game changer between project mortality and immortality, then the continuous acquisition of knowledge about phenomena is propitious to a project's success. In other words, if the advanced knowledge of PM complexity, nonlinearity, and uncertainty is essential to PM, then the relationship between phenomena and the achievement of business or project objectives can be positive, negative, or none. Proposition 7 added that if knowledge workers are the sources of sustainable competition, then effective, efficient, and knowledge practitioners can offset the relationship between complexity, uncertainty, chaos, and a project's success or immortality (Coff and Raffile, 2015). Knowledge is the total of knowledge capital and human capital required to convert mortality to immortality. The objective of knowledge acquisition can be PPGE-based micro training, PPGE-based meso training, PPGE-based macro training, and continuous training and learning.

Lundy and Morin (2013) and Reich et al. (2013) indicated deeper knowledge and an effective application of knowledge about phenomena determine the power and strength to effect positive change within project, program, and globally oriented organizations. It also helps reduce the failure (mortality) rate of complex projects. The depth of knowledge about phenomena will further enable practitioners to become knowledgeable employees able to self-organize, self-manage, self-sustain, interconnect, and collaborate.

Moreover, the research proposition stated that if the new constructs or neologisms expand PM theoretical boundaries, the extant theory must expand to accommodate the neologisms; otherwise, a superior theory should help PM practitioners understand the new PM phenomena' complexity' nature more effectively. As Table 6 indicates, the new theory guides practitioners to sustaining organizational success by focusing on comprehensive understanding and knowledge about PPGE phenomena.

Research participants who had worked in the seven industries described in Table 7 expressed the importance of a new theory in the following way:

> "Without good and virtuous theory, the project management discipline will be incoherent, misguided, and project management, as we know it, will die. The new theory will stabilize the often complex, chaotic, and uncertain PM market due to PPGE efforts. I don't believe the current PMBOK edition (5 or 6) fully explains, describes, and predicts failure or success. Theory matters especially good ones; it provides a system by which one can predict stakeholders' effects and behavior. It is a key to good practice. It optimizes performance and as well as guidance."

There were others, about 6 participants, who expressed mixed views about the idea of developing a new PM theory: "I do not know for sure. I think theory can influence or impact global-based organizations. I don't think it matters enough. But they may see the value if they have exposure. If the application of project management theory applies carefully, the likelihood of success will be high. Only those (like myself) who are interested in understanding how the profession is evolving are even aware of PM theory."

Emergent Theoretical Benefits

Research Question 7. What challenges have PM practitioners experienced due to PPGE efforts?

Proposition 7. If knowledge workers are the sources of sustainable competition, then effective, efficient, and progressive knowledge practitioners can offset the relationship between complexity, uncertainty, chaos, and a project's success or immortality.

The literature review and most of the research participants agreed that a new theory would help practitioners link PPGE constructs to practical realities by creating internal consistency among PPGE constructs. The significance of translating theory into practical application (PA) cannot be overstated; it transforms abstract concepts into concrete realities (Maranon and Pera, 2015). To sustain a realistic outcome from translating theory into practice depends on compatibility between the theory and phenomena it describes, explains, and predicts (Wilkinson et al. 2015). Studies show that when theory and practice are aligned and compatible, they produce tangible and satisfactory outcomes (Herbert et al., 2013). Through PPGE efforts, the PM domain has expanded, stretching across academic sciences, industries, and borders (Rijke et al., 2014).

Table 7
Q7: PPGE Impact on PM Practitioners

Theme	Frequency	%
Increases pressures of optimizing stakeholders' value	41	37
It makes business activities complex and uncertain	32	29
Decreases project completion rate	18	16
Increases market jolts and hacking activities	7	6
There is little link between PM theory and PM efforts	8	7
Requires knowledge beyond the PMBOK	6	5

Note. N = 112

Projectification transforms an organization to govern and operate based on PM theory and methodology (Godenhjelm et al., 2014). Programmification integrates PM and program functions and strategies in managing projects (Rijke et al., 2014). Globalization is the growth and intensification of market boundaries, stakeholders, and interdependencies across borders (Bodislav et al., 2015; Vongprasuth and Choi, 2014). These expansion and amalgamation efforts have concomitantly enlarged the complexity, nonlinearity, and uncertainty of PM. Unfortunately, PM's extant theory and methodology have not kept pace with the dictates of these emergent, evolutionary, and intricate phenomena. This has limited the capacity of PM theory to translate PPGE-based organizational activities into practical realities.

The translation of theory into PA enables researchers or institutions to achieve concrete results (Maranon and Pera, 2015). The enlargement of the field of PM through PPGEs, for instance, has increased the complexity and uncertainties of PM discipline (KapsaliBrowaldh, 2012; Vongprasuth and Choi, 2014). Thus, PM professionals are obligated to perform strategic and task-oriented operations and interconnect and collaborate with a plethora of components. They also must confront socioeconomic issues, technological, legal, cultural, and linguistic impediments, along with uncertainties spanning across multiple territorial jurisdictions.

To fully understand this complicated, interconnected web of complex realities, PM practitioners are required to link theory to practice (Thamhain, 2013). Walker (2014) asserted that the use of theory would cease if it remains isolated from practice. Kumar and Antonenko (2014) stated that irrespective of the dichotomous relationship between practice and theory, they coexist. As shown in Table 7, most respondents indicated that a good theory increases organizational values; it guides practitioners to translate theory into practical phenomena:

> "[PPGE efforts] are actively involved in helping practitioners in translating PPGE framework into success stories. It (PPGE) affects methodol-

ogy and decision-making. It (PPGE) will increase practitioners' areas of competencies and responsibilities. They [PPGE efforts] require understanding and knowledge beyond the PMBOK; knowledge of PPGE efforts makes PM practitioners better understand complex projects including stakeholders' behaviors and the economic pressures of optimizing stakeholders' value."

A good number of respondents held mixed views about the challenges practitioners have experienced due to PPGE efforts:

"[The current PM theory] provides tools, templates, standards, training, and certifications to help practitioners complete projects consistently. A good theory with no one to apply it is worse than an ok theory with someone making use of it. People normally don't follow theoretical guidance. Maybe that is why most projects fail. There is little link between the current PM theory and PM efforts to translate theory into practice. PM theory coupled with experience goes hand in hand in putting theory into practice. PMBOK provides guidelines; most practitioners rarely follow them."

They're also about a few participants who responded in this way:

"I don't think PPGE efforts affect common projects. Not very well. The focus has been on reporting findings or developing models, but the transition from those to practical advice is lacking."

Evaluation of Findings

The research propositions and questions guided the study. The study focused on collecting empirical evidence from experienced PM practitioners to support developing a new PM theory due to PPGE efforts and comparing the extant PM theory and the emergent theory aka PMT2.0. The empirical data, literature review, and participant responses were thematically arranged, organized, and grouped into three categories or slots as follows: existing PM theoretical situations, emergent theoretical outcomes, and emergent theoretical benefits (see Figure 3).

The research propositions and questions guided the study. The study focused on collecting empirical evidence from experienced PM practitioners to support developing a new PM theory due to PPGE efforts and comparing the extant PM theory and the emergent theory a.k.a. PMT2.0. The empirical data, literature review, and participant responses were thematically arranged, organized, and grouped into three categories or slots as follows: existing PM theoretical situations, emergent theoretical outcomes, and emergent theoretical benefits (see Figure 4).

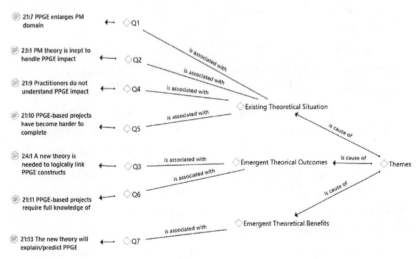

Figure 4. Participant responses summarized and grouped in three thematic slots along with their corresponding questions.

These themes and the research propositions were inextricably linked to the research propositions and questions (see Table 8). They also showed consistency between the findings and works cited. Approximately 97.5 percent of participants and works cited supported the study propositions that PPGE expansion had not the only scope crept the PM domain but limited its capacity to explain, create internal consistency among PPGE constructs completely, and predict PM phenomena. Contrary to the 2.5 percent of respondents who thought differently about developing a new theory, the study findings confirmed that PM temporality and the Triple Constraint conceptualizations were not tenable in managing complex, chaotic, uncertain, and nonlinear projects. They, therefore, supported the development of PMT2.0 to fill the ontological and epistemological gap between PM current theory and enlargement of the PM domain due to PPGE expansion efforts.

Table 8
Synthesis of Research Results

Q	Summary responses	Research Propositions
1	Due to PPGE efforts, the scope of the PM domain is enlarged	A good theory expands when its domain is enlarged
2	The enlargement incapacitates PM theory to explain and predict events	PM success is unachievable until PM theory can explain and predict PPGE constructs
3	Knowledge of PPGE impact is the sine qua non to sustainable success	Complete knowledge of PPGE constructs changes PM mortality to immortality
4	PPGE expansion integrates permanent and finite operations	Permanent and finite function integration create manifold uncertainties
5	The enlargement of the PM domain makes PM success harder to achieve	Manifold uncertainties impede practitioners' efforts to achieve success

| 6 | PMT2.0 can explain and predict the behaviors of PPGE constructs | PMT2.0 is being developed to explain and predict the impact of PPGE efforts |
| 7 | PMT2.0 will logically link PPGE constructs to practical realities | The new theory will create internal consistency among PPGE constructs |

A significant majority of participants indicated that their organizations had integrated temporary, semi-permanent, or permanent operations over the years. This contradicts PM's theoretical foundation.

Existing Theoretical Situation

This slot covers Q1, Q2, Q4, and Q5. Responses to these questions agreed with Artto et al. (2016), Bodislav et al. (2015), Gransberg et al. (2013), Nasir et al. (2015), and Vongprasuth and Choi (2014) that PPGE had transformed the PM domain by integrating PM finite functions and permanent organizational operations. They showed that the paradox of integrating temporal PM functions and permanent organizational operations had increased the complexity, chaos, uncertainty, and nonlinearity of PM function. Cases in point include construction, transportation, health care, and pharmaceutical industries, to name some examples. The extent of PPGE expansion was tested and impacted widespread in all sectors.

Table 9
PPGE Expansion Effects on Major Industries

Industry	A1	A2	A3	A4	A5	A6	A7	X	Y
Construction	H	H	H	H	H	H	H	NS	S
Education	M	H	M	H	H	M	H	NS	S
IT	H	H	H	H	H	H	H	NS	S
Health care	H	H	H	H	H	H	H	NS	S

Management	H	H	H	H	H	H	H	NS	S
Pharmaceutic	H	H	H	H	H	H	H	NS	S
Transportation	H	H	H	H	H	H	H	NS	S

Note. H = high, M = medium, L= low, S = superior, NS = not superior.

X= PM theory; Y = PMT 2.0; A1= PPGE expands PM domain; A2 = the expansion limits PM theory; A3 = PPGE constructs are complex to understand; A4 = expansion integrates finite and infinite functions; A5 = PM success is harder to achieve; A6 = a new theory is required; A7 = PMT2.0 logically links PPGE constructs to practice.

According to Table 9, X, PM theory is only superior if PPGE expansion A1, A2, A3, A4, A5, A6, and A7 are low or negligible in most or all major industries. Conversely, the emergent theory is only confirmed if A1, A2, A3, A4, A5, A6, and A7 are high in most or all major industries. The not superior performance (NS) of PM theory is supported by empirical evidence and the literature review. Chaos Report (2014, 2016) and Kaleshovska (2014) reported that only 13 percent of large government software projects succeed, 58 percent challenged, and 29 percent failed. This is translated into a perennial loss of billions of dollars.

Studies conducted in the United Kingdom, Canada, and Austria pointed out, for instance, that the application of PM's trilogy is no longer adequate or tenable to predict the performance of scope, cost, and time in a PPGE-based-complex, interrelated and interdependent-project environment (Gransberg et al., 2013; Kiridena and Sense, 2016). Deterministic relationship tests also showed that the PPGE expansion of integrating finite and infinite functions enlarged the PM domain. Put differently, when the value of A1 is increased, X or Y boundary will also increase. A probabilistic relation test also showed that if A1 is high, then X or Y is high as well.

The widespread PPGE expansion has limited the current PM theoretical capacity to fully explain, describe, and predict complex PM phenomena and made the decrease in the rate of projects' mortality onerous to achieve consistently. Some of these challenges include internal and external competitions, trade wars, currency manipulation, industrial espionage activities, data breaches, cyber warfare, legal, socioeconomic, cultural, and linguistic differences. There are also ethical and social issues that have the potential to derail organizational operations.

Research proposition 1 states that a good theory expands when its domain or boundary is enlarged and tested. The results were consistent with the literature review and participant responses. A theoretical boundary constitutes one of the essential elements of a fully developed theory. Gelso (2006) and Wacker (1998, 2004) argued that any theory that cannot completely define its boundary is not a good theory; it has an obligation to limit its domain and answer the "where" question. The "where" question explains the place and location that PM events occur in the lifecycle of the project.

PM theoretical expansion due to PPGE constructs has brought new responsibilities, approaches, and challenges to the PM domain. PM theory must equally expand to embody these neologisms; otherwise, the ability to understand stakeholders' behavior and predict, in a consistent manner, including the failure or success of PM phenomena, will be based on a hunch and that is not sustainable, especially in managing PPGE-based organizations.

Emergent Theoretical Outcomes

When asked Q6 and Q3, or how the development of new PM theory (the proposed PMT 2.0, for example) eliminates the gap between PM extant theory and the expansion of the PM domain due to PPGE, participants agreed that a new theory was needed to describe, explain, and predict the behaviors of PPGE constructs. Participants also indicated that PMT2.0 could reduce the rate of PM mortality and increase its immortality, give PM practitioners the structure to plan and control projects, and help correct deficiencies as they occur. As Gelso (2006) and Wacker (1998, 2004) defined, participants feared PM discipline would be incoherent and misguided or perished without good and virtuous theory. Moreover, most participants thought that due to PPGE-based impact, developing a new good PM theory was a fundamental building block of projects, programs, or global-based organizations. It could help organizations obtain a rational decision-making process; good theories guided every seasoned and experienced project manager.

Proposition 3, which states that a complete knowledge of PPGE constructs changes PM mortality to immortality, was overwhelmingly supported by respondents and the literature review. Lundy and Morin (2013) and Reich et al. (2013) and most respondents agreed that knowledge of PPGE constructs was the game changer between project mortality (failure) and immortality (sustainable success). The higher the knowledge, the better the results (see Appendix O). PMT 2.0 is developed to guide practitioners to acquire accurate and advanced knowledge about stakeholders. Its core plank is that superficial or reductionist knowledge cannot provide an in-depth understanding of complex phenomena. The higher the knowledge about PM phenomena, including people, equipment, software, hardware, and things-the better the chance of achieving sustainability or immortality.

Emergent Theoretical Benefits

On the question of what challenges PM practitioners have experienced due to PPGE efforts, participants stated a mismatch between theory and PPGE phenomena. There was a need to develop a new theory to guide practitioners to create internal consistency between PPGE constructs and PM theoretical foundation. Participants and the literature review also indicated that when a theory and practice are aligned, the synergy produces positive results (Herbert et al., 2013). Discourse on the significance of translating theory into practical application is rife in literature. Gelso (2006) and Gerow et al. (2015) noted that practical application of theory is propitious to financial performance, productivity, and customer service.

To fully understand this complicated and interconnected web of complex realities, PM practitioners must link theory to practice (Thamhain, 2013). Walker (2014) asserted that the use of theory would cease if it remains isolated from practice. He indicated that irrespective of the dichotomous relationship between practice and theory, they coexist. Other significant benefits of PMT2.0 include the guidance and predictability, framework or intellectual foundation, and the basis for PM methodology that it provides practitioners in managing PPGE-based projects. To achieve a sustainable competitive edge and translate theory to practice, PMT2.0 underpins practitioners to answer five questions as follows: What and who (constructs identification)? How to know the who and what (knowledge and training)? How to implement PM phenomena (methodology, policy, and strategy)? How to add value to PM phenomena (legal and ethical compliance)? How to disclose and report information (accurate financial and meeting reports)?

PMT2.0 guides practitioners to understand PPGE semantics through three basic conceptualizations explained in a five-step process (see Appendix F). The elements of this tripartite conceptualization are as follows: projectification, programmification, and globalization escalation (PPGE), complex, chaotic, uncertain, and nonlinear phenomena (CCUNP), and mortality (failure). The tripartite formulation is consistent with study proposition 4, which states that if knowledge is the game changer between project mortality and immortality, then the continuous acquisition of knowledge about phenomena is propitious to a project's success. In other words, if the advanced knowledge of PM complexity, nonlinearity, and uncertainty is essential to PM, then the relationship between phenomena and the achievement of business or project objectives can be positive, negative, or none (see Appendix H). Approximately 99.9 percent of participants espoused that knowledge of PPGE impact on PM phenomena is the sine qua non to sustainable success. Walker (2014) averred that a good theory must explicitly indicate how events are measured.

Summary

A multiple-case study research design method was used to gather empirical data from 112 participants. The data stemmed from participants' feelings, experiences, and points of view during the interview to confirm or disconfirm the need to develop a new PM theory due to PPGE expansion and compare PM theory and the emergent theory PMT2.0. The strengths of a multiple-case study included the application of surveys, interviews, and archival documents. The study religiously implemented the research protocol and procedure that the IRB and NCU approved to ensure trustworthiness.

The study used multiple control mechanisms to test the existing and emergent theories, including literature review, research propositions, empirical data, the essential elements of the theory, and a good theory's virtues. The study frequently used the necessary and sufficient conditional measures, including the evaluation processes' triangulation. These multiple testing mechanisms ensured the credibility, transferability, dependability, and confirmability of the research results. ATLAS.ti 8 was used to create codes, themes, and quotations from the literature review, participants' responses, the essential elements of the theory, and good theory virtues.

In response to Q1, Q2, Q4, and Q5, the participants and literature review agreed that the PPGE had enlarged the PM theoretical foundation, integrating permanent and finite operations. The expansion of the PM domain made PPGE-based organizational success harder to achieve. This was evident by the mediocre rate of complex project performance across industries (Chaos Report, 2016, Kaleshovska, 2014).

The complex nature of the construction, education, health care, information technology, management, pharmaceutical, and transportation industries has exacerbated the already critical issues that these industries confront (see Table 9). Salient among these vital issues are cost, schedule, hyper-competition, funding, market vicissitudes, cyber terrorism, hacking, regulatory compliance, disparate ideological incompatibility, conflicting aspiration, political rivalry, and stakeholders' s resistance (see Appendix K). A durable solution to any of these manifold PM problems requires comprehensive collaboration, negotiation, and, sometimes, political will among diverse and disparate organizations and systems across frontiers. The marked absence of an effective PM's existing theory to fully explain and predict PM phenomena' success and failure due to PPGE expansion efforts created an ontological, as well as epistemological, fissure between PM current theory and enlargement of PM domain due to PPGE expansion efforts.

Regarding Q3 and Q6, approximately 97.5 percent of participants and works cited supported the development of PMT2.0 capable of meeting the criteria of the four essential elements of theory and virtues of a good theory. Participants also agreed that a complete knowledge of PPGE constructs is the sine qua non to sustainable success. Moreover, from the findings documented in this study, the application of PMT 2.0 will guide PM practitioners from across various industries to link PPGE constructs to practice. The virtue of creating internal consistency among constructs enables practitioners to make accurate and predictable claims. It is also constituting a foundation for effective and efficient PM methodology.

Finally, in response to Q7, namely, what challenges have PM practitioners experienced due to PPGE efforts, participants agreed that PMT2.0 would undergird PM practitioners to optimize PM success. They overwhelmingly perceived PPGE constructs' knowledge as a game changer between success and failure, which is the core tenet of PMT2.0, which states that knowledge practitioners can change the relationship between complexity and success. Effective, efficient, and effective collaboration among stakeholders can promote dialogue and sharing of information. This can enable practitioners to resolve issues, create harmony among complex units, and create innovative and sustainable or win-win solutions to complex projects and chaotic situations.

CHAPTER 5

Implications, Recommendations, and Conclusions

Overview

What the promoters of project management fields, namely, the International Project Management Association (IPMA), the Project Management Institute (PMI), the Association for Project Management (APM), and the French Project Management Association (AFITEP), have aspired and predicted decades past about PM expansion, seems to occur unabated. APM membership is approximately 22,000 individuals and 550 corporate members, and IPMA has 70 member-states. PMI alone has 740,000 certified professionals and 470,000 members from 207 countries and territories. A glut of PM jobs is created annually across industries and frontiers. PMI estimated the creation of 87.7 million PM-oriented jobs in 2027 (Project Management Institute [PMI], 2017). Investment opportunities in project management have spiraled, along with the PM concept's conscientization and institutionalization. PM is considered the catalyst for infrastructural development, everyday work organizational format in major sectors, and a panacea to bureaucracy, inefficiency, and ineffective use of resources. PM's contribution to world GDP in 2027 is estimated to be US $20.2 trillion (Project Management Institute [PMI], 2017).

While PM has become the zeitgeist of infrastructural development, PM is also bittersweet. Despite its geometric expansion, the tremendous investment opportunities in the PM field, along with a luring demand for PM professionals, its track record along with the rate of maximizing the return on capital is, on average, mediocre (Karlsson, 2013). A plethora of literature reviews corroborates this view. Chaos Report (2014, 2016) and Kaleshovska (2014), for instance, reported that only 13 percent of large government software projects succeeded, 58 percent challenged, and 29 percent failed, a perennial loss of approximately billions of dollars.

The PM domain expansion due to projectification, programmification, and globalization escalation (PPGE) has integrated PM time-based functions and permanent organizational operations, making PM functionalities more complex, uncertain, chaotic, and nonlinear. Jensen et al. (2016) indicated that about 42 percent of European firms transformed their organizations into project-based entities in four years. Unfortunately, PM extant theory has not only failed to recognize the impact of this paradox on organizational governance but was also unable to keep pace with the dictates of these emergent, evolutionary, and intricate neologisms. The mismatch between the current PM theory and PPGE has created an ontological and epistemological gap (Bergman et al., 2013; Maranon and Pera, 2015). This hiatus has also added to the litany of PM's pathologies. The research participants passionately believed that the PM theory of triple constraint and its prescriptive approaches were not tenable in managing PPGE-based organizations.

Today, projects are managed within or in association with permanent or semi-permanent organizations executing PM-proven concepts and concomitantly performing the mundane business or organizational functions (Artto et al., 2015; Lindsey et al., 2016). Moreover, a globalized project-based organization requires a web of networking and interconnected stakeholders located across numerous frontiers. This makes understanding PM's current domain philosophical or theoretical basis arduous but imperative (Bodislav et al., 2015; Vongprasuth and Choi, 2014). Studies indicated that PMP certification was necessary but insufficient to manage PPGE-based organizations (Starkweather and Stevenson, 2011). This has rendered PM's theoretical foundation limited and incapable of describing, explaining, and predicting the success and failure of PPGE-projects efficiently and consistently.

The literature abounds with descriptions of PM pathologies and taxonomy of project fiascos with little or no discourse on its etiologies. Al-Ahmad et al. (2009) and Johnson et al. (2015) outlined over fifty project failures and identified theories developed to serve as panaceas to PM doldrums. PM-associated organizations involved in promoting PM works worldwide have also proposed sundry ways, including the Organizational Project Maturity Model (OPM3) to improve managing complex projects (Alami, Bouksour, and Beidouri, 2015). Irrespective of these rescue efforts, the rate of project mortality or failure remains unabated.

Since business management and PM fields are practical disciplines, what is considered a good and virtuous theory must demonstrate the real-life application in addressing these challenges and meet the criteria of the four essential theoretical components. These elements are the precise definition and description of the phenomena in question, identification of its domain and boundary, the establishment of relationships among its constructs, and predictive capability of events that may impact a project's mortality or immortality (Naor et al., 2013).

The study's purpose was to develop a new PM theory due to PPGE expansion efforts and compare the current PM theory and emergent theory, aka PMT2.0. Data collection and analysis achieved two primary goals: gathering and analyzing empirical data accurately and impartially. The data collected were based on the research protocols that IRB and NCU approved. Participants were selected from PM practitioners who were chapter members of the Project Management Institute (PMI), including other project management organizations. They had worked in the construction, education, health care, information technology, management, pharma, or transport industry (see Appendix N).

Participants were not eligible if they were not 24 or older, college graduates, had not acquired a minimum of six months of expe-

rience managing aspects of projects, programs, or global-based organizations, or not fluent in reading and writing English. Participants
were not selected based on gender; instead, they were purposely targeted because their experience and knowledge of project management (PM) phenomena provided empirical evidence to confirm or
disconfirm the emergent theory or the extant theory. Partially eligible
participants, particularly those who offered incomplete answers, did
not read, understand, and sign the Consent Form, were excluded
from the study.

Multiple case study design was appropriate for the study. It
helped the researcher focus on gathering data and comparing those
data from disparate units located in multiple sites or industries (Yin,
2009, 2014). It also helped the study collect data from peer-review
articles, archival records, interviews, open-ended survey questionnaires, and direct and indirect participant observation. The study
inextricably linked the propositions and research questions to the
study objective.

The findings supported the development of PMT2.0 deemed
capable of defragging PPGE constructs, establishing internal consistency among them, and guiding PM practitioners to describe,
explain and predict PPGE-based phenomena. They showed that
lack of understanding and knowledge of PPGE constructs makes
achieving a project objective susceptible to mortality (failure). It also
demonstrated that the more practitioners understood and learned
about complex, uncertain, chaotic, and nonlinear PM phenomena,
the better the chance of converting the specter of mortal projects into
immortal successes.

Moreover, compared to the PM extant theory, participants
found PMT2.0 to meet the essential elements of theory and good
theory virtues and capable of logically linking PPGE constructs,
creating internal consistency among them, and serving as a stabiliz-
ing tool for the PM market through the application of its three-step
conceptualization and formulation. This is explained in five steps,
and it is intended to guide practitioners to change complex, uncertain, chaotic, nonlinear PM phenomena to a sustainable competitive
advantage (see Appendix M).

The research study's contribution to literature constitutes its development of PMT2.0. The new theory's theoretical base can resolve the ontological and epistemological fissure between the extant PM theory and PM domain expansion due to PPGE efforts. This increases the complexity, uncertainty, chaos, and nonlinearity of managing projects, programs, and organizational objectives. The integration of temporary and permanent functions and how that paradox has bemused PM practitioners about the effects of PPGE constitutes a case in point. Another unveiling of note was that the PM domain's impact is widespread. The complex, uncertain, chaotic, and nonlinear nature of PPGE has adversely impacted construction, education, health care, information technology, management, pharmaceutics, and transportation industries (see Appendix K). Put differently, PPGE impact will continue to have theoretical, governing, socioeconomic, legal, environmental, and cultural implications worldwide in decades to come.

Besides, the complexity of PPGE's expansion of the PM domain spurred concerns among participants. They indicated that managing PPGE-based projects requires a profound knowledge of PPGE constructs, including stakeholders' behavior that inhabits multiple communities across different frontiers. The findings revealed that a good and virtuous PM theory is essential in achieving organizational objectives sustainably. It guides practice and underpins practitioners to unambiguously understand PPGE constructs more clearly so that they can make accurate predictions about PM phenomena.

However, to effectively predict the success and failure and establish a logical internal consistency and reliability, the constructs must interconnect and interdepend. Since a theory operates in a milieu and not in a vacuum, it must be compatible and aligned with its boundary and contextualization. Swanson and Chermack (2013) explained that a theory could hurt an organization or a society if it is not aligned to practice. Still, the synergy can produce positive results if reciprocal and aligned (Herbert, Guadiano, and Forma, 2013).

A multiple case study method seeks to answers the how and why questions, excluding how many questions. The lack of cause-and-effect relationship among case study constructs has led many experts to presume that qualitative research results are susceptible to subjectivity (Baxter and Jack, 2008; Jackson, 2012). Moreover, unlike single case research that generally describes a case unit of analysis in detail and is often parsimonious, multiple case study is limited to providing detailed analyses of case study units of analysis (Eisenhardt and Graibner, 2007; Yin, 2003). Identifying disparate and common patterns across case study units of analysis across multiple sites facilitates emergent theory evaluation. It is based on criteria such as data trustworthiness, credibility, transferability, dependability, and confirmability (De Massis and Kotlar, 2014; Yin, 2014).

The chapter discusses five essential topics: the first is an overview of the chapter. It sums up the research study problem, purpose statements, method, theoretical frameworks, limitations, and ethical issues. The second is the study implications. It provides detailed interpretative accounts of the research study findings. It also ensures that the research contribution is aligned to existing literature and relevant to theoretical development. The third topic consists of practice recommendations, focusing on how the results can apply to real-world situations, how significant they are and how they support the problem statement. The fourth is recommendations for future research. It discusses how the research results spur new developments worthy of future research investigation in the PM domain or management sciences in general. The fifth is the conclusion. It recaps the problem that was investigated and the significance of the results.

Implications

The study asked respondents seven open-ended questions and an average of two additional probed questions related to the expansion of the PM domain due to PPGE expansion efforts and, compared to PM extant theory, the development of a new theory, aka PMT2.0. The findings supported the new theory's growth due to PPGE expansion efforts being complex, chaotic, uncertain, and nonlinear. This has limited PM's extant theoretical capacity of describing, explaining, and predicting the extent of the successes or failures of PPGE phenomena. This was consistent with theoreticians, scholars, scientific definition of theory, the essential elements of the theory, and virtues of a good theory. Gelso (2006) and Wacker (1998) espoused that a good theory is supposed to have a boundary. When a new constructor idea emerges that expands or redefines it, the boundary should expand to accommodate the new concept. Otherwise, the theory will be incapable of thoroughly describing, explaining, and predicting the new construct's behavior. The research questions are paired with their corresponding propositions.

Further, the study asked participants to share their views about the impact of the new theory on PM practice and the significance of knowledge in achieving sustainability in executing PPGE-based organizational activities. The implications of participants' responses or the findings are presented in three categories: existing PM theoretical situation, emergent PM theoretical outcomes, and emergent PM theoretical benefits. Each slot will provide a summary highlighting findings that are deemed significant or contradictory to the research propositions. The existing PM theoretical situation covers questions 1, 2, 4, and 5. It provides a brief narrative of the research problem or gap that the research study intends to resolve. The emergent PM theoretical outcomes slot covers questions 3 and 6. The emergent PM theoretical benefits slot addresses question 7. It identifies a viable solution that adds significant value to theory and practice. Put differently, the category of participants presents the implications of the results anecdotally.

The Existing Pm Theoretical Situation (Q1, Q2, Q4, and Q5)

Proposition 1. If PM theory meets the four essential theoretical elements and good theory virtues, then PM's theoretical boundary will expand due to PPGE efforts.

Q1. How do PPGE efforts broaden the scope of the PM domain and impact the application of PM theory?

Respondent responses about PM theoretical boundary, whether the expansion of PPGE has enlarged PM domain, were determined in question 1. While 7 participants believed PPGE efforts have not significantly impacted their respective organizations, about 93 percent thought otherwise. The majority thought that PPGE had become the disruptive innovation, exigency for strategic changes in public and private organizations, and engine of growth and competitiveness in the 21st Century.

No primary industry is entirely spared from the impact of PPGE expansion efforts; they increased the complexity of technology use, organizational structure, environmental factors, culture, and information. It has ushered in an epoch marked by hyper-competition and increased opportunities and risks, increased the number of stakeholders with conflicting aspirations and rivalries, and geometrically increased the demand for practitioners associated with project management across the globe. PMI (2017) reported that from 2017 through 2027, 2.2 million PM-associated jobs would need annually.

While projectification transforms an organization to govern and operate based on PM theory and methodology (Godenhjelm et al., 2014), programmification integrates PM temporary functions and long-term strategies in managing projects and programs (Rijke et al., 2014). Globalization expands the growth and intensification of market boundaries, stakeholders, and interdependencies across borders (Bodislav et al., 2015; Vongprasuth and Choi, 2014). It also breeds hyper-competition and multiplies organizational risks. These expansion efforts have concomitantly enlarged the complexity, chaos, uncertainty, and nonlinearity of PM.

Moreover, the first question's findings demonstrated significant unveiling about actual PPGE impacts on the PM domain. Participants agreed that PPGE expansions had integrated the simultaneous running of temporary and permanent organizational operations, making project undertakings more complex, multifaceted, and harder to manage. This has opened the floodgates for various tasks that organizations must perform, including dealing with disparate socioeconomic and legal systems, handling global stakeholders' pressures, and confronting multiple resistant factors across frontiers.

The findings indicated that the PM phenomena' complexity due to PPGE efforts was widespread and replicated in the construction, education, health care, information technology, management, pharmaceutic, and transportation industries. The impacts of PPGE expansion were found to be directly correlated to PM domain expansion. The higher the PPGE activities, the more they expand the PM domain, and the more complex PM works become in all PPGE-based industries. Moreover, the more difficult, chaotic, uncertain, and nonlinear PM phenomena become due to PPGE efforts, the more incapacitated PM current theory becomes. The evidence showed that PM trilogy and lifecycle conceptualizations, as applied most in less complex PM milieus, were impractical in managing PPGE-based projects. This was also supported by a triangulation of peer review articles, seminal works, and reference materials. The findings suggested, besides a few that thought otherwise, that PPGE expansion efforts had increased market opportunities as well as risks.

The enlargement of the PM domain, however, raised epistemological concerns about PM theoretical capability. PM theory of temporality diametrically opposes the permanent basis upon which PPGE-based organizations operate. They perform a temporal function in parallel with the permanent operation.

Finite activities include the pursuit of management by objective (MBO) that delivers predetermined outputs, deals with short-range activities, defines each activity and function, performs temporary undertakings such as planning finite projects, scheduling, controlling, and monitoring projects. PM uses the Iron-Triangle and Earned Value Management concepts such as planned value, actual cost, and planned value to forecast or measure specific, predictable tasks (Artto et al., 2015; Godenhjelm et al., 2014; Rijke et al., 2014).

Arvidsson (2009) indicated that applying concepts such as time, task, team, and transition creates a profound difference between permanent and temporary functions. Studies show that scramble disruptions can occur when a project continues to separately maintain its short-term goal and an enterprise's long-term objective (San Cristóbal, 2015). Soderlund and Muller (2014) indicated the complex nature of the London 2012 Olympics and the Heathrow Terminal 5 projects, for instance, was a base of failure to achieve cost, time, and quality objectives. Arvidsson (2009) asserted that an understanding of PM temporal function's coexistence and permanent organizational operation improves PM performance. Jerbrant (2013) and (Johnson et al. (2016) warned that unless a new theory is developed to explain the knowledge gap between PM discipline and new advancements in the PM field, success in managing projects will continue to dwindle.

The permanent function contains planning, organizing, leading, and controlling scarce organizational resources (Kuura et al., 2013). It consists of executing a strategic plan, handling increasing global stakeholders' pressures, driving organizational change, operating in a hypercompetitive climate, and sharing a plethora of information across frontiers. It also comprises adapting to complexity, uncertainty, nonlinear environment, managing multiple processes, methodologies and coordinating internal and external projects, programs, and disparate cross-cultural teams in many countries.

The findings also showed that the current PM theory boundary had remained unchanged despite PPGE expansion efforts. The findings, supported by theoretical tests and evaluations based on the essential components of theory and virtues of good theory, found that the extant theory failed to meet the boundary criterion (see Appendix L). This confirmed research proposition 1, which states that if a good and virtuous theory provides a full description, definition, explanation, and prediction of phenomena, PM's theoretical boundary will expand due to PPGE efforts.

Proposition 2. If full description, definition, and prediction of PM phenomena undergird PM practitioners, then a complete understanding of phenomena due to PPGE is propitious to PM success.

Q2. How do PPGE efforts limit the current PM theory's capacity to fully describe, explain, and predict complex, uncertain, and nonlinear phenomena?

The findings (supported by about 95 percent of participants) confirmed that PPGE expansion had broadened PM theoretical boundary scope, made PM activities complex and uncertain, and weakened PM current theory. The findings also indicated that it would be complicated for practitioners to achieve sustainable success until PM theory can completely describe, explain, and predict these dynamic organizational cultural changes brought about by PPGE expansion efforts. These findings are consistent with proposition one and the works cited. They explained that a theory has an obligation to those it claims to represent.

Byron and Thatcher (2016), Venkatesh et al. (2013), and Wacker (1998) agreed that for a theory to receive the approbation and validity of the scientific community, it must be able to clearly define phenomena, establish a domain or territorial limitations, create relationships among its constructs and predict events among those constructs or variables. Gelso (2006) and Wacker (1998, 2004) further indicated that it must meet the four theoretical elements' criteria and the eight virtues of a good theory for a theory to stand. The four theoretical factors consist of conceptual definition, domain limitations, relationship-building, and predictive capabilities. The virtuous theory's eight characteristics are as follows: uniqueness, parsimony, conservatism, generalizability, fecundity, internal consistency, empirical riskiness, and abstraction (see Appendix J). They explained that a theory could not be distinguishable from practice and must answer the who, what, when, how, why, should, could, and would question phenomena. The who and what outline the conceptual and theoretical constructs or variables and how to define the contextual boundaries. Why and how state the purpose and mission of the theory (Gelso, 2006). The constructs or variables must interconnect and interdepend to effectively predict the success and failure and establish a logical internal consistency and reliability.

PPGE constructs have brought new responsibilities, approaches, and challenges. PM theory must equally expand to embody those new challenges; otherwise, PM's extant theoretical foundation will continue to be weakened by the complexity that PPGE constructs foster. Further, some of the complex-to-manage factors common to PPGE-based organizations include but are not limited to hacking, cyber-security issues, political conflicts, terrorism, currency manipulation and conversion, and Intellectual Property issues. The list also contains protectionism and tariffs, local and global ethical issues, different cultures and languages, incompatible socioeconomic and legal systems, and managing diverse multinational teams.

Proposition 4. If knowledge is the game changer between project mortality and immortality, then the continuous acquisition of knowledge about phenomena is propitious to a project's success. In other words, if the advanced knowledge of PM complexity, nonlinearity, and uncertainty is essential to PM, then the relationship between phenomena and the achievement of business or project objectives can be positive, negative, or none.

Q4. How do PPGE efforts transform the PM domain and its theory?

Concerning Q4, the findings indicated (about 88 percent of participants concurred) that PPGE's transformation of the PM field of study included integrating a continuous stream of organizational operations and PM finite functions. This has made PPGE-based projects far-fetched, complex, nonlinear, and chaotic; PPGE constructs are harder to manage and predict. Despite these transformations, the findings indicated that PM theoretical support had remained limited, insignificant, invisible, or unsupportable. However, 88 percent of respondents are at odds with 11 percent of the participants who thought that PPGE had no transformational effects on the PM theoretical domain. Most people were either unaware of PPGE effects or did not apply PM theory to projects. The 11 percent also thought that PMBOK best practices helped to predict the failure and success of projects and that PM current theory provided a systematic and consistent methodology for managing projects.

Proposition 5. If a theory meets the criteria of a good and a virtuous theory, as measured by the criteria drawing from Gelso (2006), Harlow (2009, 2010), and Wacker (1998), then a full understanding of phenomena due to PPGE efforts will increase and as a result, translating theory into practice will be more accurate and predictable.

Q5. How do these transformational efforts impact or influence PM theory and practice?

The findings showed that about 94 percent of participants supported the research proposition 5 that PPGE's enlargement of the PM domain had contributed to making PM works complex and challenging to achieve sustainability. The PM domain expansion was also a significant factor in delaying project implementation and making large-scale projects harder to reach or translate PM theory to practice.

Solaiman et al. (2016) indicated that the PM domain is being entrenched and integrated into every aspect of academic disciplines and creating, across industries, a litany of complex and interdisciplinary constructs such as programmification, portfolio management, project management maturity model, and green project or greenality. While project management's context is expanding exponentially, PM theory remains stagnant and inertial. The literature has also shown that PM's theoretical foundation has failed to expand its scope to align with actual complex realities that managing PPGE-based projects entail. Studies show that a good theory can guide practitioners toward achieving an organization's mission and objective in a well-organized and effective way (Miles, 2012; Swanson and Chermack, 2013).

Summary

Participant responses regarding Q1, Q2, Q4, and Q5, along with literature reviews and theoretical evaluations and tests, confirmed that due to PPGE efforts, the PM domain's scope is enlarged. The enlargement has made projects more complex, uncertain, chaotic, and nonlinear; PPGE expansion integrates permanent and finite operations. This is not only contradictory to PM extant theory but has limited its capacity to describe completely, explain, and predict the success or failure of PPGE constructs. Consequently, practitioners have found it harder to manage PPGE-based projects and far-fetched to achieve organizational objectives.

The Emergent Pm Theoretical Outcomes (Q3 And Q6)

Proposition 3. If project practitioners have little or no theoretical underpinnings about complex phenomena, then translating theory into practice will become impractical or negative. This exposes innocuous undertakings to a plethora of risks and can lead to project mortality.

Q3. How do a complete understanding, description, and prediction of complex, uncertain, and nonlinear phenomena impact a project's success?

Knowledge of PPGE constructs was found (supported by 99 percent of participants) to be propitious to sustainable success in managing PPGE-based organizational operations. It empowers PM practitioners to change failure to success and better understand complex undertakings creates innovative approaches in solving complex problems. Understanding PPGE constructs were found to guide organizations to become aware of impending risks and mitigate them. Chi and Li (2016) and Dattakumar et al. (2016) indicated that knowledge and sustainable success in managing PPGE-based organizations correlate. The more relevant and knowledgeable of PPGE expansion impact, the better the chances to achieve organizational success sustainably. PM has become boundaryless and ubiquitous. To achieve success internationally requires an in-depth understanding of phenomena at the international level as well.

The findings also pointed out that practitioners can reduce or eliminate complex projects' failure rates through good and virtuous theory. It provides an understanding of PPGE construct behaviors and predictability of PM phenomena consistently. The findings further indicated that a good and virtuous theory could provide the foundation for building the path to success, explaining PM complexity, clarifying PM phenomena, and quickly identifying risky issues.

Salient among the findings worthy of note to PPGE-based practitioners was that advanced knowledge, training, and experience could change the game from organizational mortality to immortality. To maximize sustainable organizational success requires self-managed and self-sustaining knowledge workers as well as continuous learning and training. Superior skills reduce miscalculations, knowledge workers sustain competition, macro training breeds creativity and innovations, knowledge helps to know what practitioners are against and how to find better PM solutions.

Concepts found relevant to or associated with knowledge consisted of comprehensive understanding and application of knowledge of PPGE constructs, technical knowledge, adaptation, common language, and tools. PPGE-based training or education provides an understanding of complex projects, develops leadership and soft skills, and integrates theory and practice. To sustain success also requires knowledge of stakeholders' behaviors, especially those whose buy-in impacts organizational success significantly.

Another key point that the findings revealed was the corollary between PPGE constructs' knowledge and developing PMT2.0. Consistent with research proposition 3, it was found that a good theory can provide a scientific basis for discussion, consistency and predictability, and insight to a better way of doing things and critical thinking. The theory helped understand and manage complex projects, creating a common language that practitioners and stakeholders can understand, keeping everyone on the same page, and guiding practitioners to organize work activities.

Adaptation to PPGE-based organizational context and constructs was also found to be a game changer. The literature and participants espoused that PM adaptive capacity must increase; understanding the complex nature of PPGE constructs requires continuous adaption. It also requires a good PM theory that is adaptive and scalable.

Proposition 6. If the new constructs or neologisms such as PPGE expand PM territorial boundaries, the extant theory must grow to accommodate the neologisms; otherwise, a superior theory should be developed to define clearly and comprehensively describe and predict PM phenomena.

Q6. How does the development of new PM theory (the proposed PMT 2.0, for example) eliminate the gap between PM extant theory and the expansion of the project management domain due to PPGE?

About 95 percent of participants supported developing a new theory, PMT2.0, providing a full description, explanation, and PM phenomena prediction. The findings anticipated that the new theory would give a good and virtuous theoretical framework, guide practitioners' efforts to predict phenomena, broaden its domain to include PPGE phenomena, and serve as an intellectual foundation for PM methodology, practice, template, and techniques.

The PMT 2.0 boundary accommodates PPGE efforts, creates internal stability among complex, chaotic, and uncertain PM markets by providing a coherent framework to plan activities, reduce the specter of poor investment outcomes, and guide organizations to operate accurately. The findings indicated that the successful utility of PM theory 2.0 depended on dedicated practitioners who might apply it. A good and virtuous theory can guide practitioners to manage time and resources effectively. About 6 percent of participants thought that the development of a new theory was not necessary.

Although the findings are generally compatible with literature review and research propositions, there was one area where the current theory and the emergent theory fundamentally differed. This can be metaphorically divided into two philosophical persuasions: microcosm, PM's theoretical thought, and macrocosm, PMT2.0 school of thought. The microcosmists consist of reductionists and instrumentalists, and they seek knowledge through quantitative lenses. On the other hand, macrocosmists consist of idealists. They apply qualitative research methodology to understand PM realities.

The current PM theory describes phenomena as linear and deterministic, i.e., there are always cause and effect relationships between one thing and another. PM concepts such as the trilogy-the focus on a project's scope, cost, and schedule exemplify this ethos (Gransberg et al., 2013). Moreover, reductionists believe that realities break phenomena into chunks (Stam, 1996, 2000). Concepts and approaches such as the work breakdown structure (WBS), earned value management (EVM), critical path method (CPM), and program evaluation procedure technique (PERT) is reductionist implements (Project Management Institute [PMBOK Guide], 2013).

Project management, as a macrocosm, is antithetical to the static, technocratic, and prescriptive, microcosmic view. Macrocosmists view project management phenomena as holistic, nonlinear, complex, adaptive, uncertain, and beyond microcosmic thinkers' capability to understand, let alone manage, in a sustainable fashion. The plethora of project management malaise archived in the literature due to the current PM theoretical foundations' limitation is a case in point. The contextualization and conceptualization of constructs such as projectification, programmification, and globalization have further intensified and broadened the project management domain's complexity and nonlinearity. Rijke et al. (2014) highlighted the distinction between project-oriented tasks and strategic program management projects. They explained that while programmification handles different and long-duration projects, programs, and sub-projects simultaneously, project management focuses on achieving functions that have a short period to deliver or complete its objectives. Godenhjelm et al. (2014) indicated that projectification has significantly changed the public and private sectors' structures and requires a broader theoretical and practical understanding of projectification. Idealists describe and explicate complex realities from a holistic perspective instead of reductionism (Stam, 2000).

The findings showed that while most participants found PM's current valuable theory due to its prescriptive, time, cost, scope, and quality metric, they, however, thought that the microcosmic view about PPGE expansion efforts was not adequate. The findings also indicated that PM practitioners and training institutions rarely weigh the potential benefits and risks of a PM theory before practice. Connelly (2014) showed that the absence of theory could misguide practitioners.

Summary

Motivated by the absence of PM extant theory to fully describe, explain, and predict PPGE constructs, the findings regarding Q3 and Q6 showed that participants supported developing a new theory, aka PMT2.0, to explain and predict the behaviors of PPGE constructs. The findings also indicated that due to the complex, uncertain, chaotic, and nonlinear nature of PPGE constructs, participants believed that knowledge of PPGE impact is the sine qua non to sustainable success.

The Emergent Pm Theoretical Benefits (Q7)

Proposition 7. Suppose knowledge workers are the sources of sustainable competition. In that case, effective, efficient, and progressive knowledge practitioners can offset the relationship between complexity, uncertainty, chaos, nonlinearity, and a project's success or immortality.

Q7. What challenges have PM practitioners experienced due to PPGE efforts?

The findings showed that the overwhelming majority (about 99.9 percent of participants) supported developing a new theory to create internal consistency among PPGE constructs or logically link PPGE constructs to practical realities, optimize stakeholders' value, and increase project completion rates. It also showed that a good and virtuous theory could precisely measure concepts, guide the development of discoveries in the academic and scientific disciplines, provide a framework for analysis, provide a clear explanation for the pragmatic world, and serve as an efficient method for field development (Gelso, 2006; Harlow, 2009; Udo-Akang, 2012).

Connelly (2014) indicated that a practical, theoretical framework provides a launching pad from which the practitioners can operate more logically and predict how constructs behave and their behavior outcomes. A good and virtuous theory makes it easier to examine situations from different angles. That is why in the absence of theoretical concepts in PPGE-based organizations, practitioners will be lost in the wilderness and will not know which value to promote or shun.

One theme that recurs in the findings is that PPGE constructs are complex to manage. Understanding and predicting their behavior increase the chance of achieving organizational objectives and decrease the economic pressures of optimizing stakeholders' value. The lack of the PM's current theoretical capacity to face up to PPGE's complexities and uncertainties, economic vicissitudes, constant IT jolts, hacking, and industrial espionage activities creates the need to develop PMT2.0. Put differently, PPGE expansion of the PM theoretical domain has placed PM theory in limbo. While organizations perform PM's temporal functions, they also conduct their day-to-day activities on a permanent continuum. The PM theory is incapable of describing and predicting the complexities of the temporary and permanent functions' coexistence.

The literature review and bulk of participants agreed that PMT2.0 was needed to describe and explain PPGE constructs and undergird practitioners to improve PPGE-based phenomena' predictability. A key advantage of PMT 2.0 is how to achieve sustainable success in the PPGE environment via its tripartite conceptualization explained in a five-step process (see Appendix M).

Summary

The findings explain that PMT2.0 will logically link or transform PPGE constructs to practical or concrete realities. A good and virtuous theory must be compatible or relatable to problems that it tries to solve. This contradicts what 6 percent of participants expressed. They thought methodology is the only necessary and sufficient condition and, therefore, the sole panacea to PM immortality. One of PMT2.0's core conceptualizations is that methodology selection may become part of the problem rather than the solution if PM practitioners didn't know their customers, what they want, where they are, and how the project would benefit all stakeholders. Choosing the wrong project method is like trying to fit a square peg into a round hole.

The majority view, however, confirmed the literature review and the research propositions. Maranon and Pera (2015) and Wilkinson et al. (2015) noted that a realistic outcome from translating theory into practice depends on the theory's compatibility and phenomena. It describes, explains, and predicts. Studies also showed that when theory and practice are aligned and compatible, they produce tangible and satisfactory outcomes (Herbert et al., 2013).

Stam (2006) taught that theory guides practitioners from concluding merely on assumptions and surmises. What empirical data endeavor to prove is not the case under consideration, but the theory that the data intend to test and validate. Walker (2014) asserted that the use of theory would cease if it remained isolated from practice. He indicated that irrespective of the dichotomous relationship between practice and theory, they coexist (Kumar and Antonenko, 2014).

Recommendations

The weaknesses and strengths of PM theory must be examined continually, considering PPGE expansion efforts. PMT2.0 boundary incorporates PPGE constructs. It is a workable resolution to the paradox of integrating temporary tasks and permanent operations or hiring short-term PM strategists to achieve long-term organizational outcomes (Sjoblom et al., 2013). How PMT2.0 will impact PPGE-based organizations negatively or positively requires further research. PM's future sustainable successes depend on the extent of how stakeholders across frontiers will collaborate to identify what works, particularly in PPGE-based organizations. The continuous growth of PPGE will create inverse effects on the PM field of study. If every industry is projectified, programified, or globalized, this will limit PM theoretical capacity to make feasible predictions about PM phenomena. Unlike PM extant theory, PMT2.0 can equally respond to the dynamics and complexity of PPGE transformation efforts.

An organized PPGE-based education or training is perhaps the most important missing link between PPGE expansion efforts and PM theoretical foundation. While PM theory perceives a project as a temporary undertaking disengaged from the rest of the parent organizational or institutional activities, PPGE engages temporal and permanent organizational activities. This has increased the complexity, chaos, uncertainty, and nonlinearity of PM phenomena. PPGE-based training and continuous learning are the only means by which organizations can reinvent themselves in the face of PPGE's disruptive evolution.

Recommendations for Practice

PMT2.0 holds a holistic approach to achieving organizational success. It ensures that PPGE constructs and PM theoretical or philosophical foundations are aligned and that complete knowledge and understanding of PPGE constructs are catalysts to sustaining organizational competitiveness. PMT2.0 defines a project as temporary or permanent undertakings created to develop a product or provide a service to achieve a specific objective.

PMT2.0 guides practitioners to understand PPGE semantics through three basic conceptualizations explained in a five-step process (see Appendix F). The elements of this tripartite conceptualization are as follows: projectification, programmification, and globalization escalation (PPGE), complex, chaotic, uncertain, and nonlinear phenomena (CCUNP), and mortality (failure).

PPGE is defined as the predictor, mortality, the outcome, and CUUNP, the mediator. CUUNP is related to or associated with PPGE and mortality. PPGE's expansion directly impacts mortality and indirectly elevates the CUUNP level of complexity. Stated differently, the mediator explains the extent to which the predictor (PPGE) influences or controls the outcome (mortality) (Karazsia, Berlin, Amstrong, Janicke, and Darling, 2013). If the mediating effects contradict what is observed, the mediator becomes ineffective. The replication of CUUNP across construction, transportation, information technology, health care, pharmaceutics, management, and education industries determine the strength of the association between CUUNP and PPGE (see Table 9).

PMT2.0 espouses the notion that knowledge, including knowledge capital and human capital, mediates between sustainable success (immortality) and mortality. The higher the level of knowledge, training, and experience, the better the chance of the conversion from mortality to immortality (see Appendix J). The objective of knowledge acquisition can be PPGE-based micro training, PPGE-based meso training, PPGE-based macro training, and continuous training and learning. PMT2.0 guides practitioners to change mortality to immortality through its tripartite conceptualizations explained in the five-step process (see Figure 5).

The PMT2.0 step-by-step approach guides practitioners to achieve sustainable success by linking concepts or constructs to PM realities. Studies show that when theory and practice are aligned and compatible, they produce tangible and satisfactory outcomes (Herbert et al., 2013). The step-by-step guide also addresses the following questions.

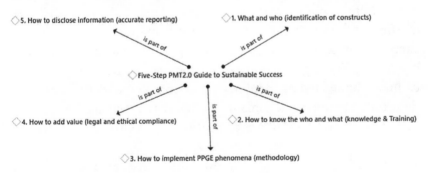

Figure 5. Five-step game changing process from mortality (failure) to immortality (sustainable success)

About PPGE-based organizations: Who and what? How do to know the who and what? How to implement PM phenomena? How do to add value to the PM phenomena? How to disclose and report information? (Creswell, 2003).

What and who (Construct and context identification)?

The first step takes practitioners through an ontological journey to identify stakeholders' anatomy, people and things that can or potentially influence or be impacted by entrepreneurial endeavors that an organization pursues, including the creation of projects to maximize the return of capital in a sustainable fashion. Investors, government, suppliers, trade associations, lobbyists, employees, communities, customers, and political groups are examples of organizational stakeholders. In PPGE-based organizations, the number of stakeholders abounds. They include global, political, economic, sociocultural, technological, environmental, and legal factors. Practitioners must organize and label them based on relevance and significance and endeavor to create active rapports with them. These constructs are complex, chaotic, uncertain, and nonlinear. The meanings, procedures, and applications of PPGE efforts cannot be isolated from their conceptualization and contextualization.

Moreover, theoretical fecundity and abstractness cover the who and what, the physical or abstract beings and realities. Their uniqueness, haecceity must be fully known to understand their behavior. Time-limited endeavors do not stymie Their existence; they are dynamic and spawning. Deep knowledge or mastery of their behavior alters the course of their nature. Learning that is adaptability-borne is better than learning that is based on prescription. Both are, however, useful in boundaryless, nonlinear, and complex undertakings. The right training about phenomena will foster theories, methodologies, strategies, or policies that are compatible, appropriate, and practical to the environment where they are applied. The wrong training or learning, on the other hand, will foster the reverse. So, the first lesson is to know stakeholders and what makes each different from any other (quiddity). The challenge is that there are hundreds of them. It is impossible to investigate them piece by piece like the reductionists. It is also perfunctory to depend on chance or common sense in dealing with multifaceted stakeholders across industries and frontiers. A good and virtuous theory, however, can guide practitioners to manage complex and highly interconnected projects consistently and methodically.

The questions who and what also constitute one of the essential elements of a fully developed theory. Any theory that cannot define its makeup and constructs, including those that are present and those that are yet to become, is not a good theory. A theory, like a country, must define its subjects thoroughly if it is to become a complete and independent state; a theory has an obligation to those that it claims to represent. PM theoretical expansion due to PPGE constructs has brought new responsibilities, approaches, and new PM domain challenges. PM theory must equally expand to embody these neologisms. For instance, if a country acquires a new territory, it must expand its boundary to include or accommodate that newly acquired territory. The new territory must become an integral part of the country; otherwise, the new territory can be susceptible to foreign encroachment. It can also weaken the relationship between the new territory and central political authorities.

To achieve sustainable success in a PPGE-based environment, project management workforce organizations must employ ethnocentric, polycentric, regiocentric, or geocentric, creditable, and respectful workforce to help, among other things, establish formal or informal communication with significant stakeholders across environments. Ethnocentric management uses its workers both at home and abroad. The polycentric workforce is native to the host country employed to manage project operations in the home country. Regiocentric personnel is hired from a variety of countries in a region. Geocentric workers are hired regardless of their citizenship. Debates may emerge regarding which of these management systems is ethically or morally superior. The strategic objective is to thoroughly identify PPGE constructs or variables, stakeholders, opportunities, and risks (Edition, 2010).

How to know the who and what (Knowledge and Training)?

The second step-by-step approach is epistemological. It guides practitioners to acquire accurate and advanced knowledge about stakeholders. The superficial, reductionist knowledge that is based solely on numbers cannot provide an in-depth understanding of complex phenomena. However, mastery of stakeholders' behaviors requires cognitive, normative, inductive, deductive, integrative, and eclectic approaches. PMT2.0 is based on the concept that knowledge can determine a project's mortality and immortality. The higher the knowledge about PM phenomena-people, equipment, software, hardware, and things-the better the chance of achieving sustainability or immortality of complex organizational objectives. The epistemological toolbox includes PPGE-based micro-knowledge or training, PPGE-based meso-knowledge or training, PPGE-based macro-knowledge or training, and continuous learning or training. The strategic aim is to hire self-organized, autopoietic, knowledge workers adaptable to changing conditions.

How to implement PM phenomena (methodology, policy, and strategy)?

The third step-by-step approach focuses on choosing the right methodology to achieve success. To do so most accurately requires choosing a methodology only after mastering step 1 and step 2. In other words, detailed identification of PPGE constructs and comprehensive understanding of the most influential and relevant stakeholders' behavior should precede methodology choice. Often, project practitioners' order of priority is to choose a convenient method instead of choosing the one with the most likelihood of achieving organizational objectives most cost-effectively and efficiently. Any organization that focuses on a methodology first before the "what, who, and why" of phenomena is bound to commit three fundamental errors: methodological incompatibility, lack of internal consistency, and limited or absence of predictive capability.

Methodological Incompatibility

PM method, like a theory, should be used as a precision tool to solve customers' problems. To be precisely applicable, it must be compatible or relatable to problems that it tries to solve. This is not the case for most practitioners. The methodology is the only necessary and sufficient condition and, therefore, the sole panacea to PM immortality.

Moreover, while the focus of PM methodologies on the software delivery cycle, how well stakeholders are engaged in the process, and how the project teams are supposed to meet, they have disregarded the PM and IT software development project's ontological perspective market has become due to PPGE. Yadav (2016) acknowledged that globalization had shifted software development from a co-located model (onsite) to an offshore model that involves the collaboration of a network of distributed teams and developers from across international frontiers. To succeed in an offshore milieu, practitioners and stakeholders must understand the phenomena' ontological and epistemological perspectives before choosing the most appropriate methodology. The ontological perspective of PPGE asks the questions: What is PPGE? What does it constitute? Is it linear, nonlinear, complex, uncertain, and undefinable? The epistemological perspective will ask: What set of knowledge acquisitions do we need to unravel PPGE's weakness and benefit? In other words, what skill set is required to fully understand and meet PPGE-based organizational and, often, incompatible stakeholders' expectations? How do we understand the behavior, volatility, interaction, success and failure of projectification, programmification, and globalization?

Lack of Internal Consistency

When a methodology or theory does not relate or create relationships among constructs, the fusion or coherence that it needs to be effectively applied is broken. Studies conducted in the United Kingdom, Canada, and Austria pointed out, for instance, that the application of PM's trilogy is not adequate to predict the performance of scope, cost, and time in a PPGE-based-complex, interrelated and interdependent-project environment (Gransberg et al., 2013; Kiridena and Sense, 2016). Packendorf and Lindgren (2013) indicated that making project management influence and control the PPGE-based organizations constitutes a significant organizational change and should be recognized by social science communities. The upsurge of the impact of projectification, programmification and globalization endeavors integrate the operation of a permanent organization and a PM temporary function and present grave multidimensional challenges to PM practitioners. Some of these challenges include internal and external competitions, trade wars, currency manipulation, industrial espionage activities, data breaches, cyber warfare, legal, socioeconomic, cultural, and linguistic differences. There are also ethical and social issues that have the potential to derail organizational operations.

Limited or Absence of Predictive Capability

A lack of understanding of the stakeholders' behaviors and constructs due to PPGE impact does not help practitioners' ability to predict the success or failure of PM phenomena. Equally, applying concepts such as the Iron Tringle or Earn Value cannot fully predict what happens in a PPGE-based environment. To be able to use auxiliary verbs such as should, could, and would in predicting the effective implementation of specific strategic policies requires the presence of other necessary or sufficient conditions such as the who, what, how, and why.

The methodological toolbox contains the application of the most appropriate method or methods that have the most likelihood of achieving the organizational objective most cost-effectively and efficiently. The strategic objective includes achieve sustainability, eliminate rework, and doing work right the first time.

How do to add value to the PM phenomena (legal and ethical compliance)?

Compliance with ethics, Foreign Corrupt Practices Act, labor laws, liability laws, personal property laws, and regulations sensitive to local and international standards is significant. It adds value to an organization and protects its reputation. Ethical standards help business organizations curb unethical behaviors in the workplace. It is challenging to handle, especially in a global climate where security breaches, intellectual property rights violations, cyber-crimes, industrial espionage activities, and privacy violations are common occurrences. A code of ethics is required to curtail unethical activities at work. However, its success depends on the content of the codes, the frequency with which management communicates it, the quality of the communication, and how senior management will model the codes in their daily transactions and the way they behave (Kaptein, 2011). Studies show that ethical standards require the full participation of stakeholders. They cannot work in an environment where people are scared to speak out or report unethical behavior and where those who are found to breach the code of ethics are not investigated or punished. Establishing channels such as an anonymous hotline, an ombudsman, and proactive ethical enforcement agents, to name a few, can encourage whistleblowers to report unethical acts without fear of reprisals (Maginnis and Charles, 2009).

Moreover, the ethical challenge increases astronomically when a company decides to operate overseas. There the culture, ethical standards, language, illegal activities, human rights, child labor, currency differences, and litigations are different and sometimes diametrical to values. Western companies espouse (Wolfendale, 2002). Breaking through those barriers requires effective leaders to conform to the subtleties of those social and cultural areas of differences and disagreement and customize business modus operandi and services to suit local stakeholders (Shen et al., 2006).

The impact of trustworthiness on organizational leadership is enormous. Most stakeholders have not yet lost sight of the dishonesty of Enron, Arthur Anderson, and WorldCom. Businesses who do the right thing by being truthful and trustworthy about their products and services and treating stakeholders with respect and dignity can build better reputations in communities. On the other hand, the less honest or trustworthy a firm's leadership becomes, the fewer shareholders will be interested in investing or doing business with the leadership in charge (Caldwell et al., 2010). Moreover, a reputable leader with a sense of trustworthiness and integrity has a better chance of building lasting relationships with customers, developing and managing better human resources, and portraying an actual business image. Studies show that employees tend to perform exceptionally well in a work environment where trust, respect, and fairness are the rules and not the exceptions (Caldwell et al., 2010).

Clearly, there is a correlation and interdependence between leadership, trustworthiness, and ethical stewardship. The more trustworthy and ethical the business and its leaders operate, the better the reputation. A corporation with a reputation, honesty, and integrity retains customers' loyalty and shareholders' commitment continually.

The axiological toolbox includes knowledge of local, national, and international ethics or standards. The strategic objective should focus on and prioritize the application of national and local norms.

How do we disclose and report information (accurate financial and meeting reports)?

Fairly reporting financial and organizational information is a strength and not a weakness. It should be encouraged. Avoiding deception or exaggeration in writing organization activities should not be compromised. The success of public relations and marketing depends on how the company can identify the services it offers, what makes those services stand out from the crowd, who are its regular and potential customers, and what it can do best by delivering those services better than everyone else. Lying to the public through public relations and marketing stratagems such as baiting and switching, promising rebates, or opportunities that cannot be delivered, is deleterious to business success. The rhetorical toolbox should contain reporting standards, recordkeeping, and marketing strategy that truly reflect the organizational status and corporate social responsibility. Strategic objectives should focus on assessing the existing information outlets, such as websites, blogs, social media, meeting reports, and project records, to ensure compliance with specific accountability requirements and taking corrective actions when necessary or required by law.

Recommendation for Future Research

Four key conclusions stemmed from the study findings and current literature reviews that have implications for future research and practice worthy of note. Firstly, PPGE has transformed organizations into performing short-range and long-range functions expanding PM current domain beyond its theoretical capacity to describe, explain, and predict PPGE constructs completely. This will continue to have theoretical, governing, socioeconomic, legal, environmental, and cultural implications. Future researchers may wish to examine the manifold dimensions of projectification, programmification, globalization, and the theoretical impact of the conflation of temporary project and organizational activities (Godenhjelm, Lundin, and Sjoblom, 2014). Moreover, far from being anomic conceptualizations, these constructs have become the zeitgeist of our time. Delving into the impact of PPGE on time and space is a challenge to future researchers. They must ensure that the boundary between temporality and permanence is clear enough to PM practitioners and the extent to which their integration has elevated the complexity of PM phenomena to higher heights.

In addition, the novelty of PPGE is significant for discussion; PPGE constructs are coterminous to PM realities and whether one is a microcosmist or a macrocosmist is of no substance. PPGE constructs exist independent of how we feel and think. What matters is how PM practitioners understand the negative or positive impact of PPGE expansion efforts and how to convert the negative impacts into positive opportunities (Nicholas and Hathcoat, 2014). Disengaging from or blatantly ignoring discussion on these complex phenomena will continue to debase efforts required to achieve success in managing PPGE-based projects fully.

Secondly, knowledge is the game-changer between organizational mortality and immortality and should be treated as such.

Training objectives should match PPGE constructs and should answer the following questions: Who and what? How do to know the who and what? How to implement PM phenomena? How to add value to the PM phenomena? How to disclose and report information? (see Appendix M). The International Project Management Association and its federated members must collaborate with educational institutions to create terminal PPGE-based learning objectives or curricula that provide PM trainees a profound understanding of PPGE constructs.

Thirdly, PM theory is essential. PM practitioners and training institutions rarely weigh the potential benefits and risks of a PM theory before practice. Connelly (2014) indicated that the absence of theory could misguide practitioners. It should be treated as a necessary factor, if not one of the sufficient factors, in PM training and learning programs. However, in the absence of coherent relationships between the theory and PM constructs, it indeed becomes impossible to clearly predict PM phenomena (Parker et al., 2015). PM practitioners should learn to explore the significance and impact of PM theory at all PM training institutions.

PMT2.0's core theoretical foundation is not limited. It provides the answers to the who, what, when, where, how, why, should, and would questions. The use of a mixed-methods research design should be encouraged in the conduct of PPGE-based research. It does not only ask the who, what, when, where, how, why, could, should, and would questions but also employs the convergence of qualitative and quantitative methods. It triangulates, cross-validates, and juxtaposes the findings, and develops a synergistic effect for the research results (Biber and Nagy, 2010). This helps to identify errors and biases in the results quickly. It also provides researchers the capacity and latitude to fully address the nuanced PPGE-based research investigation.

CONCLUSION

Participant responses and literature reviews, and theoretical evaluations and tests confirmed that, due to PPGE efforts, the PM domain scope is enlarged. The enlargement has made projects more complex, uncertain, chaotic, and nonlinear; PPGE expansion integrates permanent and finite operations. This is not only contradictory to PM extant theory but also has limited its capacity to describe completely, explain, and predict the success or failure of PPGE constructs. Consequently, practitioners have found it harder to manage PPGE-based projects and far-fetched to achieve organizational objectives.

Motivated by the absence of PM extant theory to fully describe, explain, and predict PPGE constructs, the findings showed that participants supported developing a new theory, aka PMT2.0, to explain and predict PPGE constructs' behaviors. The results also indicated that due to the complex, uncertain, chaotic, and nonlinear nature of PPGE constructs, participants believed that knowledge of PPGE impact is the sine qua non to sustainable success.

The findings explain that PMT2.0 will logically link or transform PPGE constructs to practical or concrete realities. A good and virtuous theory must be compatible or relatable to problems that it tries to solve. This contradicts what 6 percent of participants expressed. They thought methodology is the only necessary and sufficient condition and, therefore, the sole panacea to PM immortality. Maranon and Pera (2015) and Wilkinson et al. (2015) noted that a realistic outcome from translating theory into practice depends on the compatibility between the theory and its phenomena. It describes, explains, and predicts. Studies also showed that when theory and practice are aligned and compatible, they produce tangible and satisfactory outcomes (Herbert et al., 2013).

Stam (2006) taught that theory guides practitioners from concluding merely on assumptions and surmises. What empirical data endeavor to prove is not the case under consideration, but the theory that the data intend to test and validate. Walker (2014) asserted that the use of theory would cease if it remains isolated from practice. He also noted that irrespective of the dichotomous relationship between practice and theory, they coexist (Kumar and Antonenko, 2014).

REFERENCES

Adelek, A. Q., Bahaudin, A. Y., Kamaruddeen, A., Nawanir, G., and Akindoyo, D. O. (2017). Organizational factors, construction risk management and government regulations in Nigerian construction companies: Data screening and preliminary analysis. *Innovation and Sustainability Through Governance*, 3(4), 396–409. Retrieved from www.goo.gl/D4gz4s

Ahern, T., Leavy, B., and Byrne, P. (2013, July 2). Complex project management as complex problem solving: A distributed knowledge management perspective. *International Journal of Project Management*, 32(2014), 1371–1381. doi:10.1016/j.ijproman.2013.06.007.

Al-Ahmad, W., Al-Khanfar, K., Alsmara, K., Abuleif, S., and Abu-Salem, H. (2009). A taxonomy of an IT project failure: Root causes. *International Management Review*, 5(1), 93–104. Retrieved from https://goo.gl/mGxp3G.

Alami, O. M., Bouksour, O., and Beidouri, Z. (2015). An intelligent project management maturity model for Moroccan engineering companies. *The Journal for Decision Makers*, 40(2), 191–208. doi:10.1177/0256090915590329.

Alias, Z., Zawawi, E., Yusof, K., and NM, A. (2014, January 5). Determining critical success factors of project management practice: A conceptual framework. *Procedia-Social and Behavioral Sciences*, 153(2014), 61–69. doi:10.1016/j.sbspro.2014.10.041.

Ally, M., Cleveland-Innes, M., and Wiseman, C. (2010). Managing complex distance education projects in telework environment. *Journal of Distance Education*, 24(1), 1–20. Retrieved from https://goo.gl/shMCa5.

Almeida, M. V., and Soares, A. L. (2014, August 28). Knowledge sharing in project-based organizations: Overcoming the information limbo. *International Journal of Information Management, 34*(2014), 770–779. doi:10.1016/j.ijinfomgt.2014.07.003.

Alves, A., Sousa, S., Moreira, F., and Carvalho, A. A. (2016). Managing PBL difficulties in an industrial engineering and management program. *Journal of Industrial Engineering and Management, 9*(3), 586–611. doi:10.3926/jiem.1816.

Andersen, E. S. (2015). October 20. *Do project managers have different perspectives on project management? 34*(2016), 58–65. doi:10.1016/j.ijproman.2015.09.007

Anthropoulos, L., Reddick, C. G., Giannakidou, I., and Mavridis, N. (2015, July 11). Why e-government projects fail? An analysis of the health care.gov website. *Government Information Quarterly, 33*(2016), 161–173. doi:10.1016/j.giq.2015.07.003

Artto, K., Valtakoski, A., and Karki, H. (2015, March 8). Organizing for solutions: How project-based firms integrate project and service business. *Industrial Marketing Management, 45*(2015), 70–83. doi: 10.1016/j.indmarman.2015.02.021

Arvidsson, N. (2009). Exploring tensions in projectified matrix organizations. *Scandinavian Journal of Management, 25*(2009), 97–107. doi:10.1016/j.scaman.2008.09.002

ATLAS.ti: The qualitative data analysis workbench. (2012). Retrieved from http://trainingcenter.atlasti.com

Ayayi, S. O., Oyedele, L. O., Bilal, M., Akinade, O. O., Alaka, H. A., and Owolabi, H. A. (2016). Critical management practices influencing on-site waste minimization in construction projects. *Waste Management, 59*(2017), 330–339. doi:10.1016/j.wasman.2016.10.040

Bae, S., and Patterson, L. (2014, November 1). Comparison and implications of human capital theory at the individual, organization, and country levels. *Journal of Organizational Culture, Communications and Conflict, 18*(1), 12–26. Retrieved from https://goo.gl/B3R1jc

Bakhshi, J., Ireland, V., and Gorod, A. (2016). Clarifying the project complexity construct: Past, present and future. *International*

Journal of Project Management, *34*(2016), 1199–1213. doi:10.1016/j.ijproman.2016.06.002

Barkema, H. G., Chen, X., George, G., Luo, Y., and Tsui, A. S. (2015). West meets East: New concepts and theories. *Academy of Management Journal*, *58*(2), 460–479. doi:10.5465/amj.2015.4021

Batkins, S., and Brannon, I. (2014). The Obamacare regulatory rush. *Regulation, Summer 2014*, 5–6.

Battistuzzo, F. J., and Piscopo, M. R. (2015, August 30). Global projects: A bibliometric study of international business journals. *Sao Paulo*, *10*(2), 31–45. Retrieved from http://intenext.espm.br

Battistuzzo, F. J., and Piscopo, M. R. (2015, July 2015). Global projects: A bibliometric study of international business journals. *Sao Paulo*, *10*(2), 31–45. doi:10.18568/1980–486510231–452015

Baxter, P., and Jack, S. (2008). Qualitative case study methodology: Study design and implementation for novice researchers. *Where the World Learns Qualitative Research*, *13*(4), 544–559. Retrieved from http://nsuworks.nova.edu

Bell, T. R. (2016, October 3). Visually engaged ethnography: Conducting knowledge and critical consciousness. *Journal of Media Practice*, *17*(2–3), 126–137. doi:10.1080/14682753.20 16.1248173

Bergman, I., Gunnarson, S., and Raisanen, C. (2013). Decoupling and standardization in the projectification of a company. *International Journal of Managing Projects in Business*, *6*(1), 107–128. doi:10.118/17538371311291053

Berle, A. A. (1931). Corporate powers as powers in trust [Magazine]. *Harvard Law Review*, *44*(1931).

Besteiro, E. N., Pinto, J. D., and Novaski, O. (2015, November 9). Success factors in project management. *Business Management Dynamics*, *4*(9), 19–34. Retrieved from www.bmdnamics.com

Bevilacqua, M., Ciarapica, F. E., and Giacchetta, G. (2009). Critical chain and risk analysis applied to high-risk industry maintenance: A case study. *International Journal of Project Management*, *27*(4), 419–432. doi:10.1016/j.ijproman.2008.06.006

Bland, A. M., and Roberts-Pittman, B. J. (2014). Existential and chaos theory: "Calling" for adaptability in career decision making. *Journal of Career Development*, *41*(5), 382–401. doi:10.1177/0894845313498303

Boardman, A. E., Vining, A. R., and Weimer, D. L. (2016). The long-run effects of privatization on productivity: Evidence from Canada. *Journal of Policy Modeling, xxx* (2016), 1–15.

Bodislav, D. A., Bran, F., and Iovitu, M. (2015). A review of the globalization process. *Review of International Comparative Management*, *16*(4), 471–478.

Bowen, S. A., and Zheng, Y. (2014). Auto recall crisis, framing, and ethical response: Toyota's missteps. *Public Relations Review*, *41*(2015), 40–49. doi:10.1016/j.pubrev.2014.10.017

Brahm, F., and Tarzan, J. (2015, September 9). Does complexity and prior interactions affect project procurement? Evidence from mining mega-projects. *International Journal of Project Management*, *33*(2015), 1851–1862. doi:10.1016/j.ijproman.2015.08.005

Bran, F., and Popescu, M. (2015). Information and knowledge in a global context. *The USV Annals of Economics and Public Administration*, *1*(21), 37–43.

Bredillect, C. N. (2008). Exploring research in project management: Nine schools of project management research (part 6). *Project Management Journal*, *39*(3), 2–5. doi:10.1002/pmj

Brookes, N., Butler, M., Dey, P., and Clark, R. (2014). The use of maturity models in improving project management performance. An empirical investigation. *International Journal of Managing Projects in Business*, *7*(2), 231–246. doi:10.1108/IJPRB-03-2013.0007

Brunson, K. H. (2013). Principles of administration and management functions. In E. H. Kessler (Ed.), *Encyclopedia of management theory* (pp. 2–8). Thousand Oaks: SAGE Publications

Byron, K., and Thatcher, S. M. (2016). Editors' comments: "What I know now what I wish I knew then"-Teaching theory and theory building. *Academy of Management Review*, *41*(1), 1–8. doi:10.5465/amr.2015.0094

Campbell, S. (2012). Encyclopedia of case study research. In A. J. Mills, G. Durepos, and E. Wiebe (Eds.), *Comparative case study*. Thousand Oaks: SAGE Publications.

Caro, M. D. (2015). Realism. common sense, and science. *The Monist, 98*(2015), 197–214. doi:10.1093/monist/onv006

Carvalho, M. M., Patah, L. A., and Bido, D. D. (2015, April 14). Project management and its effects on project success: Cross-country and cross-industry comparisons. *International Journal of Project Management, 33*(2015), 1509–1522. doi:10.1016/j.ijproman.2015.04.004

Celik, T., Kamali, S., and Arayici, Y. (2017). Social cost in construction projects. *Environmental Impact Assessment Review, 64*(2017), 77–86. doi:10.1016/j.eiar.2017.03.001

Charrett, D., and Loots, P. (2015). Challenges in achieving successful megaprojects. *Construction Law International, 10*(2), 18–24.

Chiu, Y. C. (2010). *An introduction to the history of project management from the earliest times to AD 1900*. The Netherlands: Eburon Academic Publishers.

Coff, R., and Raffile, J. (2015). Toward a theory of perceived firm-specific human capital. *Academy of Management Perspectives, 29*(3), 326–341. doi:10.5465/amp.2014.0112

Conforto, E. C., Salum, F., Amaral, D. C., Silva, S. L., and Almeida, L. F. (2014). Can Agile project management be adopted by industries other than software development? *Project Management Journal, 45*(3), 21–34. doi:10.1002/pmj.21410

Connell, R., Collyer, F., Maia, J., and Morrell, R. (2017). Toward a global sociology of knowledge: Post-colonial realities and intellectual practices. *International Sociology, 32*(1), 21–37. doi:10.1177/0268580916676913

Creswell, J. W. (2003). *Research design qualitative, quantitative, and mixed methods approaches* (2nd ed.). Thousand Oaks, CA: Sage Publications.

Creswell, J. W. (2014). *Research Design* (4th ed.). Thousand Oaks, CA: Sage Publications.

Cudworth, E., and Hobden, S. (2012). The foundations of complexity, the complexity of foundations. *Philosophy of the Sciences*, *42*(2), 163–187. doi:10.1177/0048393110388038

Cumming, G. (2012). *Understanding the new statistics. Effect sizes, confidence intervals, and meta-analysis*. New York: Routledge.

De Massis, A., and Kotlar, J. (2014). The case study method in family business research: Guidelines for qualitative scholarship. *Journal of Family Business Strategy*, *5*(2014), 15–29. doi:10.1016/j.jfbs.2014.007

Defense major automated information systems, S. Res. GAO, 15–282 Cong., United Sates Government Accountability Office Government Accountability Office 1 (2015) (enacted).

Doda, S. (2017). The importance of knowledge management in world information. *International Journal of Human Resource Studies*, 7(1), 52–60. doi:10.5296/ijhrs.v7il.10764

Drucker, P. F. (1999). Knowledge-worker productivity: The biggest challenge. *California Management Review*, *41*(2), 79–94.

Dul, J., and Hak, T. (2008). *Case study methodology in business research*. Burlington, MA: Elsevier.

Edition, C. (Ed.). (2010). *SKS7000-excutive concepts in business strategy*. Upper Saddle River, NJ: Prince Hall.

Eisenhardt, K. M. (2011). Building theories from case study research. In A. M. Huberman and M. B. Miles (Eds.), *The qualitative researcher's companion*. Thousand Oaks: SAGE.

Eisenhardt, K. M., and Graebner, M. E. (2007). Theory building from cases: Opportunities and challenges. *Academy of Management Journal*, *50*(1), 25–32.

Ellis, T. J., and Levy, Y. (2008). Framework of problem-based research: a guide for novice researchers on the development of a research-worthy problem. *Informing Science: The International Journal of an Emerging Transdiscipline*, *11*, 18–32.

Eriksson, P., and Kovalainen, A. (2012). Case study research in business and management. In A. J. Mills, G. Durepos, and E. Wiebe (Eds.), *Encyclopedia of case study research* (pp. 93–96). Thousand Oaks: SAGE Publications.

Eseryel, U. Y., and Eseryel, D. (2013, April 20). Action-embedded transformational leadership in self-managing global information systems development teams. *Journal of Strategic Information Systems, 22*(2013), 103–120. doi: 10.1016/j.jsis.2013.02.001

Fein, M. R. (2012). Tunnel vision: "Invisible" highways and Boston's "big dig" in the age of privatization. *Journal of Planning History, 11*(1), 47–69. doi:10.1177/1538513211425209

Feldman, M., and Worline, M. (2014). The practicality of practice theory. *Academy of Management and Education, 15*(2), 304–324. doi:10.5465/amle.2014.0356

Fenwick, T., and Dahlgren, M. A. (2015). Towards socio-material approaches in simulation-based education: Lessons from complexity theory. *Medical Education, 49*(2015), 359–367. doi:10.1111/medu.12638

Ferrero, L. (2015). Agency, scarcity, and mortality. *J Ethics, 19*(2015), 349–378. doi:10.1007/s10892–05–927–4

Field, A. (2013). *Discovering statistics using IBM SPSS statistics* (4th ed.). Los Angeles, CA: Sage Publications.

Flak, L. S., and Nordheim, S. (2016, May 15). Stakeholders, contradictions and salience: An empirical study of a Norwegian G2G effort. *Conference Paper.* doi:10.1109/HICSS.2006.436

Flyvbjerg, B. (2014). What you should know about megaprojects and why: An overview. *Project Management Journal, 45*(2), 6–19. doi:10.1002/pmj.21409

Foley, G., and Timonen, V. (2015). Using grounded theory method to capture and analyze health care experiences. *Health Services Research, 50*(4), 1195–1207. doi:10.111/1475–6773.12275

Freeman, R. E. (2010). *Strategic management: A stakeholder approach.* New York: Cambridge University Press.

Friese, S. (2014). *Qualitative data analysis with ATLAS.ti* (2nd ed.). Los Angeles

Gallo, G. (2012). Conflict theory, complexity and systems approach. *Systems Research and Behavioral Sciences, 30*(2013), 156–175. doi:10.1002/sres.2132

Garel, G. (2012, December 18). A history of project management model: from pre-models to the standard models. *International*

Journal of Project Management, 663–669. doi:10.1016/j. ijproman.2012.12.011

Gelso, C. J. (2006). Applying theories to research: The interplay of theory and research in science. In *the Psychology research handbook: A guide for graduate students and research assistants* (pp. 455–464). Thousand Oaks, CA: Sage Publications.

Gilbert, M., Ruigrok, W., and Wicki, B. (2008, September *19*). Research notes and commentaries what passes as a rigorous study? *Strategic Management Journal,* 19, 1465–1474. doi:10.1002/smj.722

Gilstrap, D. L. (2013). Quantitative research methods in chaos and complexity: From probability to post hoc regression analyses. *Complexity: An International Journal of Complexity and Education, 10*(1/2), 57–70.

Godenhjelm, S., Lundin, R. A., and Sjoblom, S. (2014, October 31). Projectification in the public sector-the case of the European Union. *International Journal of Managing Projects in Business, 8*(2), 324–348. doi:10.1108/IJMPB-05–2014–0049

Goodrick, D. (2014). *Comparative case studies* [Issue brief]. Retrieved from http://www.unicef-irc.org/km/ie/

Gottfert, E. (2015). Embedding case study research into the research context. *International Journal of Sales, Retailing and Marketing, 4*(9), 23–32.

Gransberg, D. D., Shane, J. S., and Puerto, C. L. (2013). Project complexity mapping in five dimensions for complex transportation projects. *Journal of Management in Engineering, 29*(4), 316–325. doi:10.1061/(ASCE)ME.1943–5479.0000163

Greenwald, A. G. (2012). There is nothing so theoretical as a good method. *Perspectives on Psychological Science, 7*(2), 99–108. doi:10.1177/1745691611434210

Greenwood, R., and Miller, D. (2010). Tackling design anew: Getting back to the heart of organizational theory. *Academy of Management Perspectives.*

Hagood, M. C., and Skinner, E. N. (2015). Moving beyond data transcription: Rigor as issue in representation of digital literacies. *Literacy Research: Theory, Method, and Practice, 64*(2015), 429–442. doi:10.1177/2381336915617600

Hak, T., and Dul, J. (2010). Replication. In A. J. Mills, G. Durepos, and E. Wiebe (Eds.), *Encyclopedia of case study research* (pp. 805–806). Thousand Oaks: SAGE Publications.

Hanisch, B., and Wald, A. (2012, December 12). A bibliometric view on the use of contingency theory in project management research. *Project Management Journal, 43*(3), 4–23. doi:10.1002/pmj

Harlow, E. (2010). Encyclopedia of case study research. In *Contribution, theoretical* (, pp. 1–4). Thousand Oaks, CA: SAGE Publications

Hartman, N. S., Watts, C. A., and Treleven, M. D. (2013). Appreciating the complexity of project management execution: Using simulation in the classroom. *Decision Sciences Journal of Innovative Education, 11*(4), 323–334.

Haynes, D., Bawden, D., and Robinson, L. (2016, June 17). A regulatory model for personal data on social networking services in the UK. *International Journal of Information Management, 36*(2016), 872–882. doi:10.1016/j.ijinfomgt.2016.05.012

He, Q., Luo, L., Hu, Y., and Chan, A. P. (2013, July 21). Measuring the complexity of mega construction projects in China-a fuzzy analytic network process analysis. *International Journal of Project Management, 33*, 549–563. doi:10.1016/j.ijproman.2014.07.009

Herbert, J. D., Guadiano, B. A., and Forma, E. M. (2013). The importance of theory in cognitive behavior therapy: A perspective of contextual behavioral science. *Behavior Therapy, 44*(2013), 580–591. Retrieved from www.sciencedirect.com

Herman, M. J., and Handayani, R. S. (2015, January 30). The preparedness of pharmacist in community setting to cope with globalization impact. *Jurnal Kefarmasia Indonesia, 5*(1), 57–66. doi:10.22435/jki.v5i1.4087.57–66

Holloway, W., and Jefferson, T. (2000). *Doing qualitative research differently. A free association, narrative and interview method.* London: Sage Publications.

Hsu, C., and Sandford, B. A. (2012). Instrumentation. In N. J. Salkind (Ed.), *Encyclopedia of research design* (, pp. 608–610). Thousand Oaks: SAGE Publications.

Huarng, K., and Mas-Tur, A. (2016). Turning Kurt Lewin on his head: Nothing is so theoretical as a good practice. *Journal of Business Research, 68*(2016), 4725–4731. doi:10.1016/j.jbures.2016.04.022

Jackson, S. L. (2012). *Research methods and statistics: A critical thinking approach* (4th ed.). Belmont, CA: Wadswoth Cengage Learning.

Jallow, A. K., Demian, P., and Anuma, C. (2014). An empirical study of the complexity of requirements management in construction projects. *Engineering, Construction and Architectural Management, 21*(5), 505–531. doi:10.1108/ECAM-09–2013–0084

Jalocha, B. (2012). Projectification of the European Union and its implications for public labor market organizations in Poland. *Journal of Project, Program and Portfolio Management, 3*(2), 1–16.

Jerbrant, A. (2013). A maturation for model project-based organizations-with uncertainty management as an ever-present multi-project management focus. *SAJEM Special Issue, 17*(2014), 33–51.

Johnson, N., Creasy, T., and Fan, Y. (2015). Fifteen years of theory in project management: A review. *International Journal of Construction Project Management, 7*(2), 154–166. Retrieved from https://goo.gl/W9DGm8

Johnson, N., Creasy, T., and Fan, Y. (2016). Recent trends in theory use and application and application within the project management discipline. *Journal of Engineering, Project, and Production Management, 6*(1), 25–52. Retrieved from https://goo.gl/aajjpQ

Jones, I., Brown, L., and Holloway, I. (2013). Grounded theory. In *Qualitative research in sport and physical activity*. London: SAGE Publications.

Kaiser, M. G., Arbi, F. E., and Ahlemann, F. (2014, March 31). Successful project portfolio management beyond project selection techniques: Understanding the role of structural alignment. *International Journal of Project Management, 33*(2015), 126–139. doi:10.1016/j.ijproman.2014.03.002

Kalaignanam, K., Kushwaha, T., and Eilert, M. (2013). The impact of product recalls on future reliability and future accidents: Evidence from the automobile industry. *Journal of Marketing, 77*(2014), 41–57.

Kaleshovska, N. (2014). Adopting project management offices to exploit the true benefits of project management. *Economic Development, 1*(2), 151–165.

KapsaliBrowaldh, M. (2012). Equifinality in project management exploring causal complexity in projects. *Systems Research and Behavioral Science, 30*(2013), 2–14. doi:10.1002/sres.2128

Karazsia, B. T., Berlin, K. S., Amstrong, B., Janicke, D. M., and Darling, K. E. (2013). Integrating mediation and moderation theory development and testing. *Journal of Pediatric Psychology, 39*(2), 163–173. doi:10.1093/jpepsy/jsto80

Karlsson, A. K. (2013). Politicized projects: Schedule modification as a tool for coordination between temporary interventions and long-term policies at an aid agency. *Scandinavian Journal of Public Administration, 17*(2), 13–35. Retrieved from https://goo.gl/HoASoa

Kettley, N. (2010). *Theory building in educational research.* London: Continuum International Publishing Group.

Kim, J., and Wilemon, D. (2013, March 29). Complexity and the multiple impacts on new product development: results from a field study. *International Journal of Innovation and Technology Management,* 9(6), 1250043-1–1250043-25. doi:10.1144/S0219877012500435

Kiridena, S., and Sense, A. (2016). Profiling project complexity: Insights from complexity science and project management literature. *Project Management Journal, 47*(6), 56–74. Retrieved from http://wwwpmi.org/pmj

Kumar, S., and Antonenko, P. (2014). Connecting practice, theory and method: Supporting professional doctoral students in developing conceptual frameworks. *TeckTrends, 58*(4), 54–61. doi:10.1007/s11528–014–0769-y

Kuura, A., Blackburn, R. A., and Lundin, R. A. (2013). Entrepreneurship and projects-linking segregated communities. *Scandinavian Journal of Management, 30*(2014), 214–230. doi:10.1016/j.scaman.2013.10.002

Kwak, Y. H. (2005). *The history of managing projects*. Wesport, CT: Praeger Publishers.

Kwak, Y. H., Sadatsafavi, H., Walewski, J., and Williams, N. L. (2015, June 3). Evolution of project based organization: A case study. *International Journal of Project Management, 33*(2015), 1652–1664. doi: 10.1016/j.ijproman.2015.004

Lalonde, C., and Boiral, O. (2012). Managing risks through ISO 31000: a critical analysis. *Risk Management, 14*(), 272–300. doi:10.1057/rm.2012.9

Lalonde, P., Bourgault, M., and Fedeli, A. (2010). Building pragmatist theories of PM practice: Theorizing the act of project management. *Project Management Journal, 41*(5), 21–36. doi:10.1002/pmj.2063

Lanham, H. J., Keykum, L. K., Taylor, B. S., McCannon, C. J., Linberg, C., and Lester, R. T. (2012, July 4). How complexity science can inform scale-up and spread in health care: Understanding the role of self-organization in variation across local contexts. *Social Sciences and Medicine, 93*(2013), 194–202. doi:10.1016/j.socscimed.2012.05.040

Lattimer, H. (2015). Translating theory into practice: Making meaning of learner centered education frameworks for classroom-based practitioners. *International Journal of Educational Development, 45*(2015), 65–76. doi:10.1016/j.ijedudev.2015.09.012

Lawrence, J., and Tar, U. (2013). The use of Grounded theory technique as a practical tool for qualitative data collection and analysis. *The Electronic Journal of Business Research Methods, 11*(1), 29–40. Retrieved from http://wwwejbrm.com

Lawter, L., Kopelman, R. E., and Prottas, D. J. (2015). McGregor's theory X/Y and job performance: A multi-source analysis. *Journal of Managerial Issues, XXVII*(1–4), 84–101. Retrieved from https://goo.gl/cdWk5S

Lehrer, K. (1990). *Theory of knowledge*. Abingdon, UK: Westview Press.

Lindsey, A. M., Mears, D. P., and Cochran, J. C. (2016). The privatization debate: A conceptual framework for improving (public and private) corrections. *Journal of Contemporary Criminal Justice, 32*(4), 308–327. doi:10.1177/1043986216660006

Littau, P., Jujagiri, N. J., and Adbrecht, G. (2010). 25 years of stakeholder theory in project management literature (1984–2009). *Project Management Journal, 41*(4), 17–29. doi:10.1002/pmj.20195

Liu, X. (2016, July 11). Motivation management of project-based learning for business English adult learners. *International Journal of Higher Education, 5*(3), 2016. Retrieved from http://www.sciedupress.com/ijhe

Liu, Z., Zhu, Z., Wang, H., and Huang, J. (2015, December 11). Handling social risks in government-driven mega project: An empirical case study from West China. *International Journal of Project Management, 34*(2016), 202–218. doi:10.1016/j.ijproman.2015.11.003

Lock, D. (2013). *Project Management* (10th ed.). Burlington, VT: Gower.

Love, P. E., Ahiaga-Dagbui, D. D., and Irani, Z. (2016). Cost overruns in transportation infrastructure projects: Sowing the seeds for a probabilistic theory of causation. *Transportation Research Part A, 92*(2016), 184–194. doi:10.1016/j.tra.2016.08.007

Lu, M., Wu, Z., and Meng, Q. (2015, July 31). Comprehensive development evaluation system of Asian infrastructure investment bank based on double diamond model. *Asian Journal of Industrial and Business Management, 5*(2015), 518–526. doi:10.4236/ajibm.2015.57051

Lundqvist, S., and Marcusson, L. (2014). Advertisements for ICT project managers show diversity between Swedish employers' and project management associations' views of PM certifications. *Problems of Management in the 21st Century, 9*(1), 35–57. Retrieved from https://goo.gl/fqonkJ

Lundy, V., and Morin, P. (2013). Project leadership influences resistance to change: the case of the Canadian public service. *Project Management Journal*, *44*(4), 45–64. doi:10.1002/pmj.21355

Majoor, S. J. (2016, July 1). Copying with ambiguity: An urban megaproject ethnography. *Progress in Planning*, *410*(2016), 1–28. doi:10.1016/j.progress.2016.07.001

Malbasic, I., Rey, C., and Potocan, V. (2014, June 12). Balanced organizational values: From theory to practice. *J Bus Ethics*, *2015*(130), 437–446. doi:10.1007/s10551–104–2238–0

Maltzman, R., and Shirley, D. (2010). *Green project management*. Boca Raton, FL: CRC Press.

Manca, S., and Ranieri, M. (2016). Facebook and the others. Potentials and obstacles of social media for teaching in high education. *Computers and Education*, *95*(2016), 216–230. doi:10.1016/j.compedu.2016.01.012

Maranon, A. A., and Pera, A. P. (2015). Theory and practice in the construction of professional identity in nursing students: A qualitative study. *Nurse Education Today*, *35*(2015), 859–863. doi:10.1016/j.nedt.2015.03.014

Marshall, B., Cardon, P., Poddar, A., and Fontenot, R. (2013). Does sample size matter in qualitative research? A review of qualitative interviews in IS research. *Journal of Computer Information Systems*, *54*(1), 11–22. doi:10.1080/08874417.2013.11645667

Matos, S., and Lopes, E. (2013). Prince2 or PMBOK-A question of choice. *Procedia Technology*, *9*(2013), 787–794. doi:10.1016/j.protcy.2013.12.087

Mayer, I. (2015). Qualitative research with a focus on qualitative data analysis. *International Journal of Sales, Retailing and Marketing*, *4*(9), 53–67.

Maylor, H., Brady, T., Cooke-Davies, T., and Hodgson, D. (2006, January 12). From projectification to programmification. *International Journal of Project Management*, *24*(2006), 663–674. doi:10.1016/j.jproman.2006.09.014

McCurdy, H. E. (2013, February 7). Learning from history: Low-cost project innovation in the US National Aeronautics and Space

Administration. *International Journal of Project Management,* *31*(2013), 705–711. doi:10.1016/j.ijproman.2013.001

McKusker, K., and Gunaydin, S. (2015). Research using qualitative, quantitative or mixed methods and choice based on the research. *Perfusion, 30*(7), 537–542. doi:10.1177/0267659114559116

Miles, J. A. (2012). *Management and organization theory.* San Francisco, CA: Jossey-Bass.

Miles, M. B., Huberman, A. M., and Saldana, J. (2014). *Qualitative data analysis* (3rd ed.). Los Angeles: SAGE.

Mir, F. A., and Pinnington, A. H. (2013, May 14). Exploring the value of project management: Linking project management performance and project success. *International Journal of Project Management, 32*(2014), 202–217. doi: 10.1016/j.ijproman.2013.05.012

Mitchell, G. E., and Schmitz, H. P. (2013, October 29). Principled instrumentalism: A theory of transnational NGO behavior. *British International Studies Association, 40*(2014), 487–504. doi:10.1017/S0260210513000387

Miterev, M., Engwall, M., and Jerbrant, A. (2016). Exploring program management competences for various program types. *International Journal of Project Management, 34*(2016), 545–557. doi:10.1016/j.ijprogman.2015.07.006

Muller, R., Zhai, L., Wang, A., and Shao, J. (2016, May 20). A framework for governance of projects: Governmentality, governance structure and projectification. *International Journal of Project Management, 34*(2016), 957–969. doi:10.1016/j.ijproman.2016.05.002

Naor, M., Bernardes, E., and Coman, A. (2013). Theory of constraints: Is it a theory and a good one? *International Journal of Production Research, 51*(2), 542–554. doi:10.1080/00207543.2011.654137

Nasir, M. H., Sahibuddin, S., Ahmad, R., and Fauzi, S. S. (2015, July 8). How the PMBOK addresses critical success factors for software projects: A multi-round Delphi study. *Journal of Software, 10*(11), 1283–1300. doi:10.17706/jsw.10.11.1283–1300

Negrea, A. (2012). Globalization and the identity dilemma. *Theoretical and Applied Economics*, *XIX* (2012), 93–116.

Neverauskas, B., Bakinaite, L., and Meiliene, E. (2013). Contemporary approach to the possibility of project's success increase. *Economics and Management*, *18*(4), 829–836. doi:10.5755/j01.em.18.4.5710

Nguyen, A. T., Nguyen, L. D., Le-Hoai, L., and Dang, C. N. (2014). Quantifying the complexity of transportation projects using the fuzzy analytic hierarchy process. *International Journal of Project Management*, *33*(2015), 1364–1376. doi:10.1016/j.ijprogman.2015.02.007

Nicholas, M. C., and Hathcoat, J. D. (2014). The SAGE encyclopedia of action research. In *Ontology*. London: SAGE Publications.

O'Brien, D. (2017). *An introduction to the theory of knowledge* (2nd ed.). Malden, MA: Polity Press.

Oellgaard, M. J. (2013). The performance of a project life cycle methodology in practice. *Project Management Journal*, *44*(4), 65–83. doi:10.1002/pmj.21357

Oerlemans, L., and Pretorius, T. (2014). Linking project-based production and project management temporary systems in multiple contexts: An introduction to the special edition. *SAJEMS Special Issue*, *17*(2014), 1–16. Retrieved from https://goo.gl/RJRre7

Ofori, D. F., Nyuur, R. B., and S-Darko, M. D. (2014, February 20). Corporate social responsibility and financial performance: fact or fiction? a look at Ghanaian banks. *AOSIS Open Journals*, 11. doi:10.4102/ac. v14/1.180

O'Leary, Z. (2007). The social science jargon buster. In *Instrumentalism* (pp. 139–140). Thousand Oaks, CA: SAGE Publication.

Ozer, B., and Seker, G. (2013). Complexity theory and public policy: A new way to put new public management and governance in perspective. *The Journal of Faculty of Economics and Administrative Sciences*, *18*(1), 89–102. Retrieved from https://goo.gl/5yQJQJ

Packendorf, J., and Lindgren, M. (2013). Projectification and its consequences: Narrow and broad conceptualizations. *SAJEMS Special Issues, 17*(2014), 7–21. doi:10.4102/sajems.v17i1.807

Packer, M. (2011). *Science of qualitative research.* New York: Cambridge University Press.

Padalkar, M., and Gopinath, S. (2016). Are complexity and uncertainty distinct concepts in project management? A taxonomical examination from literature. *International Journal of Project Management, 34*(2016), 688–700. doi:10.1016/j.ijproman.2016.02.009

Padgett, D. K. (2004). *The qualitative research experiences.* Belmont, CA: Cengage Learning.

Palmer, I., Dunford, R., and Akin, G. (2009). *Managing Organizational Change* (Second Edition ed.). New York, NY: Mc Graw-Hill Irwin.

Park, C., and Kang, C. (2008). Does education induce healthy lifestyle? *Journal of Health Economics, 27*(2008), 1516–1531. doi:10.1016/jhealeco.2008.07.005

Park, J., and Park, M. (2016). Qualitative versus quantitative research methods: Discovery or justification? *Journal of Marketing Thought, 3*(1), 1–7. doi:10.15577/jmt.2016.03.01.1

Parker, D. W., Parsons, N., and Isharyanto, F. (2015, February 16). Inclusion of strategic management theories to project management. *International Journal of Managing Projects in Business, 8*(3), 552–573. doi:10.1108/IJMPB-11-2014-0079

Parylo, O. (2012). Qualitative, quantitative, or mixed methods: an analysis of research design in articles on principal professional development (1998–2008). *International Journal of Multiple Research Approaches, 6*(3), 297–313. Retrieved from https://goo.gl/iN9[th]N

Patra, B. P. (2010, August 24). Moral weakness: An analysis of self-indulgent actions of CEOs Enron, WorldCom and Salyam computers. *Vilakshan, Ximb Journal of Management,* 168–180. Retrieved from http://library.ncu.edu/

Petrova, E., Dewing, J., and Camilleri, M. (2016). Confidentiality in participatory research: Challenges from one study. *Nursing Ethics, 23*(4), 442–454. doi:10.1177/0969733014564909

Pinto, J. D., Novaska, O., Antholon, R., and Besteiro, E. N. (2014). Measuring project complexity and uncertainty: Scale proposal. *Business Management Dynamics, 4*(1), 29–51. Retrieved from www.bmdnamics.com

Pitsis, T. S., Shankaran, S., Gudergan, S., and Clegg, S. R. (2014, September 13). Governing projects under complexity: Theory and practice in project management. *International Journal of Project Management, 32*(2014), 1285–1290. doi:10.1016/j.ijproman.2014.09.001

Poston, R. S., and Richardson, S. M. (2010). Designing an academic project management program: A collaboration between a university and a PMI chapter. *Journal of Information Systems Education, 11*(1), 55–72. Retrieved from https://goo.gl/MJK5Aa

Program management improvement accountability act, S. Res. S.1550, 114th Congress (2015–2016) Cong., 114–264 Office of Management and Budget 1 (2016) (enacted).

Project Management Institute. (2013). *Project management institute 2013 annual report* [Annual report]. Retrieved from www.pmi.org/about-us/~/media/PDF/Publications/PMI-2013

Project Management Institute. (2013). *Project management institute: A guide to the project management body of knowledge (PMBOK) Guide* (5th ed.). Newtown Square, PA: Project Management Institute.

Project Management Institute. (2017). *Job growth and talent gap 2017–2027.* Newtown Square, PA: PMI.

Pucciarelli, F., and Kaplan, A. (2016). Competition and strategy in higher education: Managing complexity and uncertainty. *Business Horizons, 59*(2016), 311–320. doi:10.1016/j.bushor.2016.01.003

Pugh, D. S., and Hickson, D. J. (2007). Management and decision making in organizations. In *Writers on organizations* (pp. 2–25). Thousand Oaks: SAGE Publications.

Puri, C. P. (2009). *Agile management feature driven development*. New Delhi, India: Global India Publications

Qureshi, S. M., and Kang, C. W. (2014). Analyzing the organizational factors of project complexity using structural equation modeling. *International Journal of Project Management*, *33*(2015), 165–176. doi:1016/j.ijproman.2014.04.006

Qasi, A., Quigley, J., Dickson, A., and Kiryttopoulos, K. (2016). Project Complexity and the risk management (ProCrim): Towards modeling project complexity driven risk paths in construction projects. *International Journal of Project Management*, *34*(2016), 1183–1198. doi:10.1016/j.ijroman.2016.05.008

Ramazani, J., and Jergeas, G. (2014). Project managers and the journey from good to great: The benefits of investing in project management training and education. *International Journal of Project Management*, *33*(2015), 41–52. doi:10.1016/j.ijproman.2014.03.012

Reich, B. H., Gemino, A., and Sauer, C. (2013, October 16). How knowledge management impacts performance in projects: An empirical study. *International Journal of Project Management*, *32*(2014), 590–602. doi:10.1016/j.ijproman.2013.09.004

Reis, H. T., and Judd, C. M. (2014). *Handbook of research methods in social and personality psychology* (2nd ed.). New York, NY: Cambridge University Press.

Remington, K. (2011). *Leading complex projects*. Burlington, VT: Asgate Publishing Company.

Rigby, E., Clark, J. H., and Pelika, S. (2014). Party politics and enactment of "Obamacare": A policy-centered analysis of minority party involvement. *Journal of Health Politics, Policy and Law*, *39*(1), 58–95. doi:10.1215/03616878-2395181

Rijke, J., Herk, S. V., Zevenbergen, C., Ashley, R., Hertogh, M., and Heuvelhof, E. T. (2014, February 14). Adaptive programme management through a balanced performance/strategy oriented focus. *International Journal of Project Management*, *32*(2014), 1197–1209. doi:10.1016/j.ijproman.2014.01.003

Ryan, C. (2015). Schopenhauer on idealism, Indian and European. *Philosophy East and West, 65*(1), 18–35. Retrieved from https://goo.gl/UbVY9x

San Cristóbal, J. R. (2015, February 22). The use of game theory to solve conflicts in the project management and construction industry. *International Journal of Information Systems and Project Management, 3*(2), 43–58. doi:10.12821/ijispm030203

Santos, F. M., and Eisenhardt, K. M. (2004). Multiple case study. In *the SAAGE encyclopedia of social science research methods.* Thousand Oaks: SAGE Publications.

Sauchelli, A. (2013, May 22). Life extension and the burden of mortality: Leon Kass versus John Harris. *J Med Ethics, 40*(2014), 336–340. doi:10.1136/medethics.2013.10148

Saungweme, P. W. (2015). Teaching project management at a South African higher education institution. *South African Journal of Higher Education, 29*(3), 131–149. Retrieved from https://goo.gl/usXiWc

Schmidt, T. (2016, April 4). Instrumentalism about practical reason: Not by default. *Philosophical explorations, 19*(1), 17–27. doi:10.1080/1386975.2015.1134632

Sciara, G., Bjorkman, J., Sryjewski, E., and Thorne, J. H. (2016). Mitigating environmental impacts in advance: Evidence of cost and time savings for transportation projects. *Transportation Research Part D, 50*(2017), 316–326. doi:10.1016/j.trd.2016.10.017

Scranton, P. (2014). Projects as a focus for historical analysis: Surveying the landscape. *History and Technology, 30*(4), 354–373. doi:10.1080/07341512.2014.1003164

Serrador, P., and Pinto, J. K. (2015, January 5). Does Agile work? -A quantitative analysis of agile project success. *International Journal of Project Management, 33*(2015), 1040–1051. doi:10.1016/j.ijproman.2015.01.006

Sharma, N. (2013, April 12). Theoretical framework for corporate disclosure research. *Asian Journal of Finance and Accounting, 5*(1), 183–195. doi:10.5296/ajfa.v5il.3210

Simons, H. (2012). Case study research in practice. In *Dispelling myths in case study research*. London: SAGE Publications.

Simsit, Z. T., Gunay, N. S., and Vayvay, O. (2014). Theory of Constraints: A literature review. *Proccedia-Social and Behavioral Sciences*, *150*(2014), 930–936. doi:10.1016/j.sbspro.2014.09.104

Sjoblom, S., Lofgren, K., and Godenhjelm, S. (2013). Projectified politics-temporary organizations in a public context. Introduction to the special issue. *SJPA*, *17*(2), 3–12. Retrieved from https://goo.gl/wyyVmL

Smith, K. G., and Hitt, M. A. (2002). *Great minds in management*. New York: Oxford University Press.

Smith, P. P., and Gibson, L. A. (2016). Project-based learning in colleges of business: Is it enough to develop education graduates? *New Directions for Teaching and Learning*, (145), 41–47. doi:10.1002/tl.20173

Soderlund, J., and Muller, R. (2014). Project management and organization theory: IRNOP meets PMJ. *Project Management Journal*, *45*(4), 2–6. doi:10.1002/pmj.21442

Sparks, W. L., and Repede, J. F. (2016). Human motivation and leadership: Assessing the validity and reliability of the actualized leader profile. *Academy of Educational Leadership Journal*, 20(3), 23–43. Retrieved from https://goo.gl/6dKEe6

Stam, H. (2000). Theoretical psychology. In *The international handbook of psychology*. London, England: Sage Publications

Stam, H. J. (2006). On the use of theory. *The General Psychologist*, *41*(2), 30–32. Retrieved from https://goo.gl/ht2gWi

Stam, H. J. (2010). Theory. In N. J. Salkind (Ed.), *Encyclopedia of Research Design*. Thousand Oaks, CA: SAGE Publications

Starkweather, J. A., and Stevenson, D. H. (2011). PMP certification as a core competency: Necessary but not sufficient. *Project Management Journal*, *42*(1), 31–41. doi:10.1002/pmj.2074

Sternberg, T. (2016, May 21). Water megaprojects in deserts and drylands. *International Journal of Water Resources Development*, *32*(2), 301–320. doi:10.1080/07900627.2015.1012660

Steyn, H. (2001). An investigation into the fundamentals of critical chain project scheduling. *International Journal of Project Management, 19*(6), 363–369. doi:10.1016/ S0263–7863(00)00026–0

Stone, D. L., Deadrick, D. L., Lukaszewski, K. M., and Johnson, R. (2015). The influence of technology on the future of human resource management. *Human Resource Management Review, 25*(2015), 216–231. doi:10.1016/j.hrmr.2015.01.002

Streb, C. K. (2012). Exploratory case study. In A. J. Mills, G. Durepos, and E. Wiebe (Eds.), *Encyclopedia of case study research*. Thousand Oaks: SAGE Publications.

Strosetzki, C. (2014). From the microcosm to the macrocosm: Ethos and policy in vives. *eHumanista, 26*(2014), 530–538. Retrieved from https://goo.gl/Vy1N3s

Subramanian, S. (2013). "Instrumentalism" and Friedman's methodology: A short objection. *Quality and Quality, 47*(1), 577–580. doi:10.1007/s11135–011–9480–7

Sullivan, L. E. (2009). The SAGE glossary of the social and behavioral sciences. In L. E. Sullivan (Ed.), *Epistemology*. Thousand Oaks, CA: SAGE Publications.

Sullivan, L. E. (2009). The SAGE Glossary of the social and behavioral sciences. In *Realism*. Thousand Oaks, CA: SAGE Publications

Suter, W. N. (2014). Qualitative data, analysis, and design. In *Introduction to educational research: A critical thinking approach* (pp. 342–386). doi:10.4135/9781483384443

Svejvig, P., and Andersen, P. (2014, June 28). Rethinking project management: A structured literature review with a critical look at the brave new world. *International Journal of Project Management, 33*(2015), 278–290. doi:10.1016/j.ijproman.2014.06.004

Swanson, R. A., and Chermack, T. J. (2013). *Theory building in applied disciplines*. San Francisco, CA: Berrett-Koehler Publishers.

Sweeney, P. (2002). The travails of Tyco. *Financial Executive*, 20. Retrieved from www.fei.org

Tallon, A. R. (2014). Encyclopedia of environmental change. In J. A. Mathews (Ed.), *Ontology*. Thousand Oaks, CA: SAGE Publications.

Thamhain, H. (2013). Managing risks in complex projects. *Project Management Journal*, *44*(2), 20–35. doi:10.1002/pmj

Thamhain, H. J. (2013). Commitment as a critical success factor for managing complex multinational projects. *International Journal of Innovation and Technology Management*, *10*(2013), 1–17. doi:10.1142/S0219877013500168

The standish group report. (2014). *Chaos report* [Annual report].

Thomas, G. O., Walker, I., and Musselwhite, C. (2014, June 24). Grounded theory analysis of commuters discussing a workplace carbon-reduction target: Autonomy, satisfaction, and willingness to change behaviors in drivers, pedestrians, bicyclists, and bus users. *Transportation Research*, *26*, 72–81. doi:10.1016/j.trf.2014.06.009

Trkman, P. (2010). The critical success factors of business management. *International Journal of Information Management*, *30*(2010), 125–134. doi:10.1016/j.ijinfomgt.2009.07.003

Trochim, W. M. (1989). Outcome pattern matching and program theory. *Evaluation and Program Planning*, *12*(1989), 335–366. doi:10.1016/0149–7189(89)90052–9

Turpin, Z. (2015). Melville, mathematics, and platonic idealism. *Leviathan*, *17*(2), 18–34. Retrieved from https://goo.gl/59Vs7u

Udo-Akang, D. (2012). Theoretical constructs, concepts, and applications. *American International Journal of Contemporary Research*, *2*(9), 89–96. Retrieved from http://www.aijcrnet.com

Uhl-Bien, M., Marion, R., and Mckelvey, B. (2007). Complexity leadership theory: Shifting leadership from the industrial age to the knowledge era. *The Leadership Quarterly*, *18*(4), 298–318. doi:10.1016/j.leaqua.2007.04.002

Valle, M., and Lanier, D. (2016). Teaching Microsoft Project in project management classroom: The dream home project exercise. *Business Education Innovation Journal*, *8*(2), 133–145. Retrieved from http://www.beijournal.com

Valle, M., and O'Mara, K. J. (2015). Adaptive project management: A classroom exercise to explore the fundamentals of Agile (SCRUM). *Journal of the Academy of Business Education*, *16*(2015), 257–275. Retrieved from https://goo.gl/i1b3wu

Van Rijnsoever, F. J. (2017). (I can't get no) saturation: A simulation and guidelines for sample sizes in qualitative research. *PLOS ONE*, *12*(7), 1–17. doi:10.1371/journal.pone.0181689

Venkatesh, V., Brown, S. A., and Bala, H. (2013). Bridging the qualitative-quantitative divide: guidelines for conducting mixed methods research in information systems. *MIS Quarterly*, *37*(1), 21–54. Retrieved from https://goo.gl/pdrNtr

Verdam, M. G., Sprangers, M. A., and Oort, F. J. (2013, May 14). Significance, true and proof of p values: reminders about common misconceptions regarding null hypothesis significance testing. *Qual Life Res*, 5–7. doi:10.1007/s11136–013–0437–2

Verweij, S. (2014). Achieving satisfaction when implementing PPP transportation infrastructure projects: A qualitative comparative analysis of the A15 highway DBFM project. *International Journal of Project Management*, *33*(2015), 189–200. doi:10.1016/j.ijprman.2014.05.004

Vishual, A. (*2012*). Qualitative and quantitative research: Paradigmatic differences. *Global Education Journal*, 2012(4), 155–163. Retrieved from https://goo.gl/59Vs7u

Vogt, W. P., Garner, D. C., and Haeffele, L. M. (2012). *When to use what research design*. New York, NY: A Division of Guilford Publications.

Vongprasuth, T., and Choi, C. G. (2014, October 7). Globalization, foreign direct investment, and urban growth management: Policies and conflicts in Vientiane, Laos. *Land Use Policy*, *42*(2015), 790–799. doi:10.1016/j.landusepol.2014.10.003

Wacker, J. G. (1998). A definition of theory: Research guidelines for different theory-building research methods in operations management. *Journal of Operation Management*, *16*(4), 361–385. doi:10.1016/S0272–6963(98)00019–9

Walker, S. (2014). A mutual reshaping: Theory and practice. *Studies in Art Education*, *55*(4), 267–269. Retrieved from https://goo.gl/HAA3oT

Walton, M. (2014, April 13). Applying complexity theory: A review to inform evaluation design. *Evaluation and Program Planning*, *45*(2014), 119–126. doi:10.1016/j.evalprogplan.2014.04.002

Westhorp, G. (2013). Developing complexity-consistent theory in a realist investigation. *Evaluation, 19*(4), 364–382. doi:10.1177/1356389013505042

Whetten, D. A. (1989). What constitutes a theoretical contribution? *Academy of Management Review, 14*(4), 490–495. doi:10.5465/AMR.1989.4308371

Whitehead, P. M. (2017). Goldstein's self-actualization: A biosemiotic view. *The Humanistic Psychologist, 45*(1), 71–83. doi:10.1037/hum0000045.

Wiener, M., Mahring, M., Remus, U., and Sanders, C. (2016). Control configuration and control enactment in information systems projects: Review and expected theoretical framework. *MIS Quarterly, 40*(3), 741–774. Retrieved from http://www.misq.org.

Wilkinson, D. M., Smallidge, D., Boyd, L. D., and Giblin, L. (2015). Students' perceptions of teaching methods that bridge theory to practice in dental hygiene education. *The Journal of Dental Hygiene, 89*(5), 330–337. Retrieved from https://goo.gl/2AsczK.

Williams, T. (2015). Identifying success factors in construction projects: A case study. *Project Management Journal, 47*(1), 97–112. doi:10.1002/pmj.21558.

Wilman, K. (2016). Case study: An airport ground transportation management programme and contractor. *Journal of Airport Management, 11*(1), 48–57. Retrieved from https://goo.gl/ynPQjc.

Winter, M., and Smith, C. (2006). *Rethinking project management* [Final Report]. Retrieved from www.rethinkingpm.org.uk: http://www.rethinkingpm.org.uk.

Wood, P., and Butt, G. (2014). Exploring the use of complexity theory and action research as frameworks for curriculum change. *Journal of Curriculum Studies, 46*(5), 676–696. doi:10.108/00220272.2014.921840.

Woodside, A. G. (2014). Embrace perform model: Complexity theory, contrarian case analysis, and multiple realities. *Journal of Business Research, 67*(2014), 2495–2503. doi:10.1016/j. jbusres.2014.07.006.

Wray, K. B. (2015, September 30). The methodological defense of realism scrutinized. *Studies in History and Philosophy of Science, 54*(2015), 74–79. doi:10.1016/j.shpsa.2015.09.001

Wysocki, R. K. (2014). *Effective complex project management. An adaptive agile framework for delivering business value.* Plantation, FL: J. Ross Publishing.

Yadav, V. (2016). A flexible management approach for globally distributed software projects. *Global Journal of Flexible Systems Management, 17*(1), 29–40. doi:10.1007/s40171–015–0118–9.

Yakovleva, A. (2014). Methodological aspects of project techniques selection for innovation project management. *International Journal of Innovation,* 2(1), 18–31. doi:10.2139/ssrn.2513793.

Yang, L., Huang, C., and Hsu, T. (2013, January 22). Knowledge leadership to improve project and organizational performance. *International Journal of Project Management, 32*(2014), 40–53. doi:10.1016/j.ijproman.2013.01.011.

Yilmaz, K. (2013). Comparison of quantitative and qualitative research tradition: epistemological, theoretical, and methodological differences. *European Journal of Education, 48*(2), 312–325. doi:10.1111/ejed.12014.

Yin, R. K. (2009). *Case study research: Design and methods* (4th ed.). Thousand Oaks, CA: SAGE.

Yin, R. K. (2012). Case study protocol. In A. J. Mills, G. Durepos, and E. Wiebe (Eds.), *Encyclopedia of case study research.* Thousand Oaks: SAGE Publications.

Yin, R. K. (2013). Review Essay. *Canadian Journal of Action Research, 14*(1), 69–71. Retrieved from https://goo.gl/mqp4U9.

Yin, R. K. (2014). *Case study research: Design and methods* (5th ed.). Los Angeles, CA: SAGE.

Ylijoki, O. (2016). Projectification and conflicting temporalities in academic knowledge production. *The Theory of Science, XXXVIII* (1), 1–26.

Yoshikawa, H., Weisner, T. S., Kalil, A., and Way, N. (2013). Mixing qualitative and quantitative research in developmental science:

uses and methodological choices. *Qualitative Psychology*, 1, 3–18. doi:10.1037/2326.1. S.3.

Yung, P. (2015). A new institutional economic theory of project management. *Journal of Business Economics and Management*, *16*(1), 228–243. doi:10.3846/16111699.2012.748689

Zhao, Y. (2014, August 12). Interpreting innovation dynamics with complexity theory. *International Journal of Innovation and Technology Management*, *11*(5), 1–18. doi:10.1142/S0219877014500357.

APPENDICES

Appendix A
Research Protocol

Purpose and objective: The purpose of the research is to explore the development of a new project management theory and to examine the differences between the existing PM theory and the emergent PMT 2.0. Our goal is to know what you think about the impact of projectification, programmification, and globalization on the project management domain; how you feel about developing a new project management theory that will thoroughly explain and predict the success or failure of managing projects across multiple industries.

Procedures: Participants who meet the following research recruitment criteria will be invited to participate:

Participants will read and sign the Informed Consent Form

The primary researcher will contact the participant to make an appointment for the interview

Participants will determine when the interview will be held and by what channel (face to face, phone, email, Skype, etc.) It will take approximately 35 minutes to fill out the survey questionnaire or participate in the interview.

Research participants will incur no cost to participate.

Participants (21 years of age and over) who are project management practitioners or chapter members of Project Management Institute; fluent in reading and writing English; worked in any construction, health care, information technology, management, pharmaceutics, and transportation industry to participate in the research study.

Participation is entirely voluntary.

Participants are at liberty to withdraw from the research or refuse to answer any questions except when a participant's response had been submitted and anonymously recorded.

Research design and sampling: Onsite participants will fill out surveys or answer the interviewer's questions during the interview. The interviewer will collect the completed surveys and recode the analysis interview.

There are no risks involved in participating in the research. The research may end in August 2017. The finite date, however, will depend on the IRB approval.

Data analysis: Data collected via onsite and online surveys will be securely protected. Participants' names will be de-identified to prevent a person's identity from being connected to the information that they have provided to the research. The original surveys, recordings, emails, cover letters will be destroyed in conformity with IRB regulation.

Moreover, in compliance with Northcentral University, Federal and Institutional Review Board, and research ethics and regulations, participation and personal data will remain anonymous and confidential. Only the principal dissertation committee members will have access to the research data.

Reporting Procedures: The research report's presentation will take place at Northcentral University during the dissertation defense. The report will include a summary of data, findings, study limit or delimit, and recommendations. Personal responses and information that participants provided to the research team will be kept confidential and stored on a secure server. These data will eventually be destroyed according to IRB protocol.

If Northcentral University accepts, the primary researcher will entertain no objection to invite any participant who wants to participate in the final dissertation defense ceremony. Upon request, a summary of the research results will be made available to participants.

This dissertation research is being conducted by an avid doctoral candidate, guided and mentored by connoisseurs and experts in research methodologies, technology, and business management in dissertation research.

Appendix B
Informed Consent Form

Introduction: My name is Abu Fofana. I am a doctoral student at Northcentral University. I am undertaking a research study to develop a new project management theory due to the increase of project, program, and global business activities. These activities are many, very difficult, and uncertain. As a result, the current project management theory cannot fully describe, explain, and predict them. The purpose of the research is to develop a theory that will define, explain, and predict the behavior of these activities. This research study is a part of my doctoral degree program. I invite you to participate.

Activities: To take part in this research study, you must fulfill the following:

1. Permit us to find out if you can take part in the study.
2. Give us your contact information to tell you about the research study.
3. Know that we will protect your privacy and confidential information.
4. Read and sign the Informed Consent Form and return it to us.
5. Know that we will call you to set a date, place, and time to interview you.
6. Know that we will also call, email, and ask you to complete the survey questionnaires online.
7. Know that the questions are open-ended.
8. Know that the interview or the online survey questionnaires will take about 35 minutes to complete.
9. Know that participants who live in the United States will have face-to-face or phone interviews.
10. Know that approximately 101 participants will complete the online open-ended interview questions. Only 11 participants will be phone or face-to-face interviewed conducted mainly in the North American region.

Eligibility: To take part in this research study, you must fulfill the following:

1. Be a chapter member of the Project Management Institute (PMI)
2. Be a member of other project management organizations related to the Project Management Institute.
3. Have worked in the construction, health care, information technology, management, pharma, or transport industry.
4. Be 24 or older.
5. Be a college graduate.
6. Have more than six months' experience working for projects, programs, or global organizations.
7. Be fluent in reading and writing English.

You are not eligible to participate in this research if you:

1. Are a child, prisoner, pregnant woman, or mentally disabled person
2. Do not read, understand, and sign the Informed Consent Form.

Risks: Risks that you may encounter in taking part in the research are minimal. Some of the obvious risks may include the discomfort associated with being interviewed or completing online survey questionnaires. The research data, including your contact information, may also be hacked or lost. The study will do its best to minimize the loss of data by, among other things, using Norton Security suit to secure data, protect the identity, and make sure the computer and hard drives are password protected and stored in a secure location. Moreover, you can skip responding to an interview question or withdraw from the research study altogether.

Benefits: There is no direct benefit for taking part in the study.

Volunteering: Taking part in the study is voluntary. You have the right to leave at any time.

Confidentiality: To keep your information confidential and protect your privacy, the study will use alphanumeric or letter codes to identify you. This will keep your real name separate from your answers.

Audiotaping: If you agree, I can record the interview. You can still take part in the research if you do not want me to record the interview.

Please sign here if I can record you:

Confidentiality: I will use tight physical security, endpoint malware detection, and network protection efforts to protect recorders, hard drives, and electronic files from hackers. The research team will destroy all data after seven years.

Only the researcher and his supervisor will have access to the research data.

Contact Information: If you have questions, you can contact me at A.Fofana4100@email.ncu.edu. 804.901.1830 /973.727.6782. My dissertation chair's name is Dr. Patrick McNamara. You can contact him at pmcnamara@ncu.edu. 888–327–2877, ext.6080. You can also contact the Institutional Review Board at irb@ncu.edu or 1–888–327–2877 ext. 8014.

Signature: Singing this Informed Consent Form means that you have read, understood, and agreed to take part in the research study.

Participant Signature	Printed Name	Date

Researcher Signature	Printed Name	Date

Appendix C
Cover Letter

Dear Participant,

I wish to invite you to participate in my doctoral dissertation research study entitled, "*Exploring New Theory in Project Management Field Due to Projectification, Programmification and Globalization Escalation*." The research will explore creating a new project management theory, aka PMT 2.0, due to PPG escalation efforts. I am enrolled in the School of Business and Technology Management, specializing in project management at Northcentral University. The purpose of the research is twofold: to develop a new PM 2.0 that will fully match the new PM phenomena that projectification, programmification, and globalization have created. The study will also examine the differences between the existing PM theory and the emergent PMT 2.0.

This survey, along with the interview questions, has been approved by the Institutional Review Board (IRB) of Northcentral University. Your participation in this research project is completely voluntary. By completing and submitting this survey, you are indicating your consent to participate in the study. Participation will remain anonymous and confidential. Only the principal dissertation committee members will have access to the research data. There is no risk associated with participation. There is no direct reward for participation. We, however, feel that helping the research achieve its objective may particularly benefit project management practitioners; project management theory can have a negative or positive impact on an organization or a society. This is evident by the successes and failures of public and private projects all around us.

If you agree to participate in this project, please complete the questionnaire and return it as soon as possible. It should take approximately 35 minutes to complete. If you have any questions about this project, please contact Abu Fofana at A.Fofana4100@email.ncu.

edu, Dr. Patrick McNamara at pmcnamara@ncu.edu, or the IRB of Northcentral University at irb@ncu.edu.

Thank you for participating.

Sincerely yours,

Abu Fofana
PhD candidate and principal investigator

Appendix D
Recruiting Flyer

Introduction. I am a doctoral student at the School of Business and Technological Management at Northcentral University, San Diego, California. I am specializing in project management. As partial fulfillment of the degree of Doctor of Philosophy requirements, I am launching a dissertation study entitled, *"Exploring New Theory in Project Management Field Due to Projectification, Programmification and Globalization Escalation."* I invite you to participate.

What is the study about? The dissertation research study aims to develop a new PM theory 2.0 (PMT2.0) and compare the current project management theory and the proposed PMT2.0.

Who can participate? Potential participants must:

1. Be 24 or older.
2. Be a college graduate.
3. Be fluent in reading and writing English.
4. Be project management personnel.
5. Be chapter members of the Project Management Institute (PMI).
6. Have worked in construction, health care, information technology, management, pharmaceutical, or transportation industry.
7. Have also acquired more than six months of experience in managing aspects of project, program, or global-based organizations.

What's involved? Participants will sign an informed consent form. They will also complete an online survey or take part in an interview. A face-to-face or a phone interview will occur mainly in North America. It will take about 35 minutes to complete the online survey or the interview. Approximately 101 participants will complete the online open-ended interview questions. Only 11 participants will be phone or face-to-face interviewed, conducted mainly in the North American region.

What are the benefits of participating? There is no direct reward for participation. However, helping the research achieve its objective may benefit project management practitioners; project management theory can positively impact an organization or a society.

What are the risks? Risks that you may encounter in taking part in the research are minimal. Some of the apparent risks may include the discomfort associated with being interviewed or completing online survey questionnaires. The research data, including your personal information, may also be hacked or lost. The study will do its best to minimize the loss of information by using Norton Security to secure data, protect identity, and make sure the computer and hard drives are password protected and stored in a secure location. Moreover, you can skip responding to an interview question or withdraw from the research study altogether.

Confidentiality. To keep your information confidential and protect your privacy, I will use a fake name to identify you. This will keep your real name separate from your answers.

If you wish to volunteer and participate in the study (now or later) or have questions about the research, please contact the primary investigator or his advisor and chairman of the Dissertation Research Board.

Abu Fofana, Primary Researcher   Dr. Patrick McNamara,
                                 Dissertation Chairman

A.Fofana4100@email.ncu.edu   pmcnamara@ncu.edu and the
973–707–6782/   IRB of Northcentral University
804–901–1830   at irb@ncu.edu.

Appendix E
Research Interview Guide

Introduction: (Shaking hands). Hello Mr./Mrs._____. My name is Abu Fofana. I am a doctoral student at the School of Business and Technological Management at Northcentral University, San Diego, California, specializing in project management. I am conducting a dissertation study on the title: *Exploring new theory in the project management field due to projectification, programmification, and globalization escalation.* Volunteers must be project management practitioners and Project Management Institute chapter members who have worked in construction, health care, information technology, management, pharmaceutics, and transportation. Knowing that you are a bonfire member of the PMI local chapter and a project management practitioner, we think it is a great idea to interview you so that you can share your view, experience, and personal thoughts with us.

Purpose: The purpose of the dissertation research is to explore the development of a new project management theory, PMT 2.0, that will fully match the new project management realities that projectification, programmification, and globalization have created and to examine the differences between the existing PM theory and the emergent PMT 2.0.

There is no direct reward for participation. We, however, feel that helping the research achieve its objective may particularly benefit project management practitioners; project management theory can have a negative or positive impact on an organization or a society. This is evident by the successes and failures of public and private projects all around us.

The interview will take about 35 minutes. If you are not available now, you can call or email us at A.Fofana4100@email.ncu.edu to make an appointment.

I. Questions about expanding projects, programs, and global stakeholders

1. I want to begin by asking you to introduce yourself and the organization you serve briefly. This should include your name, year(s) of experience in the project management field.

   a) What do the terms projectification, programmification, and globalization mean to you or your organization?

   b) How do they make your organization?

   c) Can you explain how the implementation of these expansion efforts has impacted your organization?

2. Experts in theory development say a good project management theory is supposed to have a boundary, coherent relationship among variables or constructs, a reason to exist, and the ability to predict organizational objectives' success and failure. They explain that the boundary can be enlarged or expanded when a new term or idea emerges that changes the theoretical domain. Based on this assessment, do you think the current project management theory thoroughly explains, describes, and predicts the failure and success of a project? Please explain.

II. Impact of project, program, and global effects on project management success

3. How does the enlargement of the project management domain because of projectification, programmification, and globalization expansion affect the way your project and organizational objectives are executed?

   a) In your experience, do these changes make it easier or harder to achieve your business or project objectives? Please explain.

4. Describe your experiences in managing a project-based, programed-based, and global-based organization?
   a) Do you think that knowledge of PM realities can help achieve success in managing projects for your organization? Please explain.

III. Project Management Theoretical Support

5. How has the current project management theory provided you or your organization the theoretical support required to understand and predict the failure and success of projects? Please explain.
6. Describe why and how project management theory is significant for your organization and the field of project management.

IV. Knowledge of the functions and tasks that practitioners perform.

7. Some project management scholars have criticized the current project management theory for being narrow regarding projectification, programmification, and globalization expansion efforts in project management.
   a) Do you think expanding the tasks and functions that practitioners perform due to projectification, programmification and globalization have equally expanded the current PM theoretical base?
   b) Do you think the impact of these expansion efforts is aligned with the current project management theory?
   c) Does the current project management theory fully explain, describe, and predict PM phenomena' success and failure?

8. Do you think developing a new project management theory is necessary due to projectification, programmification, and globalization efforts?
   a) Describe how a new theory will impact your organization (positively or negatively)
   b) What kind of value will a new theory bring to your organization or the project management domain?

V. Translating project management theory into practice

9. How does the current project management theory underpin and guide translating project management theory into practice?
10. How does the application of project management theory impact project-based, program-based, and global-based organizations?

VI. The importance of theory to project management practitioners

11. Do you think PM theory matters to project management practitioners?
12. How does a theory guide project management practice? Does it reduce or increase the chances of project success or failure? Please explain.

VII. Relationship between a theoretical understanding of project management phenomena and the increasing rate of project failure

13. Do you think knowledge of the expansion of the project management domain due to projectification, programmification, and globalization increases the chance of completing projects on time? Please explain.

14. What do you think about a theory that fails to fully describe, explain, and predict failure and success of phenomena?

    a) What makes an inadequate and ineffective theory? Please explain.

Closing: Thank you, Mr./Mrs. _____ for the interview. We appreciate your participation. We are going to transcribe the interview. Will it be ok if we call you to verify certain information that you have given us today? Thank you again for your participation.

Appendix F
Phone Recruitment Script

On the Phone:

Hello, my name is Abu Fofana. I am a doctoral student at Northcentral University. I am undertaking a research study to develop *a new project management theory due to the projectification, programmification, and globalization escalation.* The dissertation research study aims to develop a new project management theory 2.0 (PMT2.0) and compare the current project management theory and the new theory. This research study is a part of my doctoral degree. I am calling to ask if you would be willing to let me interview you. It should take about 35 minutes to complete the interview. Taking part in the study is voluntary. There are no benefits, and the risks are minimal. Your data will remain confidential. Only the principal dissertation committee members will have access to the research data.

Who can participate? Potential participants must:

1. Be 24 or older.
2. Be a college graduate.
3. Be fluent in reading and writing English.
4. Be project management personnel.
5. Be chapter members of the Project Management Institute (PMI).
6. Have worked in construction, health care, information technology, management, pharmaceutical, or transportation industry.
7. Have also acquired more than six months of experience in managing aspects of project, program, or global-based organizations.

What's involved? Participants will sign an informed consent form. They will also complete an online survey or take part in an interview. A face-to-face or a phone interview will occur mainly in North

America. It will take about 35 minutes to complete the online survey or the interview. Approximately 101 participants will complete the online open-ended interview questions. Only 11 participants will be phone or face-to-face interviewed, conducted mainly in the North American region.

What are the benefits of participating? There is no direct reward for participation. However, helping the research achieve its objective may benefit project management practitioners; project management theory can positively impact an organization or a society.

If you would be interested, we can set up a time now. You can also call and let me know later what time will be convenient for you for the interview.

If you have questions, please call 973–707–6782/804–901–1830 or email me at <u>A.Fofana4100@email.ncu.edu</u>. Thank you for participating.

Appendix G
Research Propositions

Proposition 1: If a good and virtuous theory provides a full description, definition, explanation, and prediction of phenomena, then PM's theoretical boundary will expand due to the projectification, programmification, and globalization Escalation (PPGE) efforts.

Proposition 2: If an increase in project success rate depends on an understanding of PM theoretical foundation, then knowing the effects of PPGE will increase the chances of project success. In other words, if a theory is positively associated with PM success, then PM success will increase as the result of changing PM theory to accommodate PPGE efforts.

Proposition 3: If a deep understanding and macro knowledge of phenomena reduce or eliminate the specter of complex, uncertain, and chaotic project, program, and globally interconnected business operations, then a micro or minimal understanding of what the PM domain has become due to PPGE efforts will not achieve organizations' overarching objectives. In other words, the less the knowledge of complex and chaotic problems, the more amiss and dismal the completion rate.

Proposition 4: Compared with extant PM theory, if PMT 2.0 fully meets the criteria of a good and virtuous theory, then PMT 2.0 will undergird practitioners' efforts to increase the rate of project success.

Proposition 5: If a theory meets the criteria of a good and a virtuous theory, as measured by the criteria drawing from Gelso (2006), Harlow (2009, 2010), and Wacker (1998), then a full understanding of phenomena, due to PPGE efforts, will increase and as a result translating theory into practice will be more accurate and predictable.

Proposition 6: If the new constructs or neologisms such as PPGE expand PM territorial boundaries, the extant theory must expand as well to accommodate the neologisms; otherwise, a stronger and more superior theory should be developed to provide a better understanding of the nature of the new PM phenomena (Coff and Raffile, 2015). In other words, if a good and virtuous theory provides full description, definition, explanation, and prediction of phenomena, then PM success rate will increase because of knowledge and application of a good and virtuous theory. On the contrary, if a theory does not provide full definition, explanation, and prediction of phenomena, then PM success rate will decrease because of knowledge and application of incomplete and nebulous theory.

Proposition 7: If knowledge workers are the source of sustainable competition, then the effective, efficient, and continuous acquisition of knowledge about PM phenomena can offset the relationship between complexity, uncertainty, chaos, and a project's success or immortality (Coff and Raffile, 2015).

Appendix H
Demographic Characteristics

Demographic Characteristics of Participants (N=112)		
Characteristic	N	%
Minimum age at the time of survey 24 or above	112	100
College graduate (minimum)	112	100
PMP certified	109	97
Minimum experience of six months in managing PPG-based project (s)	104	93
Average experience in 3–6 multiple industries	101	90
Location		
Africa	5	4
Asia	9	8
Europe	19	17
Middle East	9	8
North America	61	54
South America	9	8
Industry		
Construction	18	16
Education	21	19
Health care	9	8
Information Technology	33	30
Management	20	18
Pharmaceutics	4	4
Transportation	5	4
Others	1	1

Appendix I
Comparison between PM Theory and PMT2.0

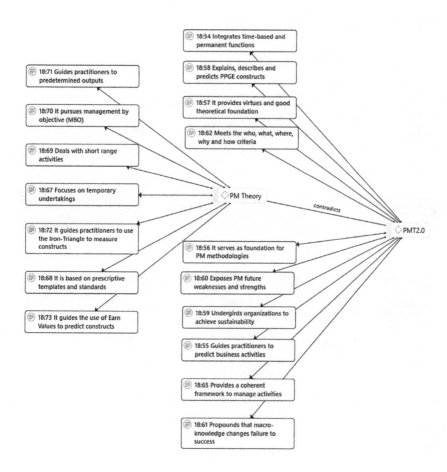

Appendix J
Virtues of Good Theory

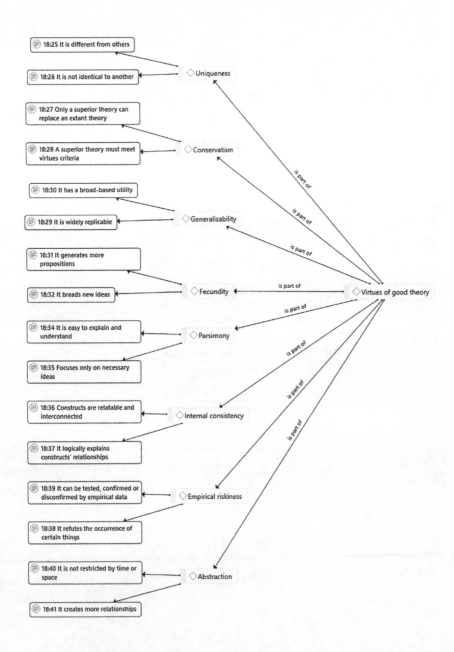

Appendix K
PPGE Expansion Impact

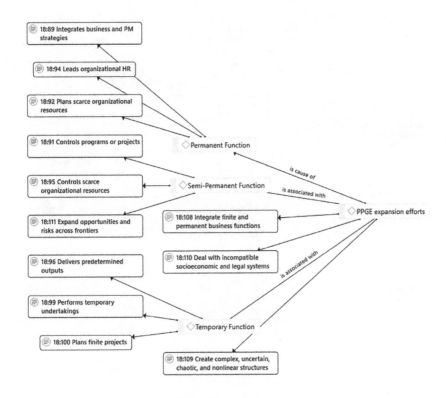

Appendix L
Theory Testing Control Chart

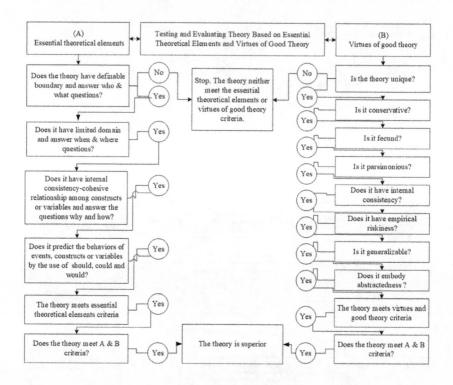

Appendix M
How PMT 2.0 Undergirds PM Practitioners to Achieve Sustainability: A Five-Step Approach

What and who (Construct and context identification)? How to know the who and what (Knowledge and Training)? How to implement PM phenomena (methodology, policy, and strategy)? How to add Value to PM phenomena (legal and ethical compliance)? How to disclose and report information (accurate financial and meeting reports)?

Step 1: What and who?	Ontological toolbox	Strategic objective
PPGE constructs are complex, chaotic, uncertain, and nonlinear. PPGE meaning and application cannot be isolated from its conceptualization and contextualization.	Employ knowledgeable, diverse, ethnocentric, polycentric, regiocentric, or geocentric workforce	Thoroughly identify PPGE constructs or variables, stakeholders, opportunities, and risks
Step 2: How to know the who and what?	Epistemological toolbox Macro and continuous learning/ training	Strategic objective Retain or hire knowledge practitioners
Take a universal approach to understand stakeholders' behaviors.		

Step 3: How to apply it?
Deep knowledge of step 1 and step 2 precedes the choice of methodology

Methodology toolbox
Waterfall, SCRUM, Agile, and Prince2, to name few examples

Strategic objective
Knowledge of project environment should go before a method selection

Step 4: How to add Value to the PM phenomena?
Compliance with laws and regulations sensitive to local standards is significant

Axiological toolbox
Application of local, national, and international ethics or standards including Oxley or Dad-Frank

Strategic objective
Fully comply with appropriate laws and regulations

Step 5: How to report it?
Fairly reporting and avoiding deception or exaggeration should not be compromised

Rhetorical toolbox.
Business reports should conform to standards that reflect good CSR

Strategic objective
Focuses on accurate and truthful reporting

Appendix N
Description of Units of Analysis

Industry	Description Due to PPGE Impact	Critical Issues	References
Construction	Imbued with diverse stakeholders, legal, socioeconomic, cultural environmental, safety, political, technology complexities	Cost, quality, design, risk, environmental, workplace safety and regulatory factors	(Peleskei et al., 2015; Allen et al., 2015; Tan et al., 2015; He et al., 2014)
Education	Complex due to PPGE and collaborative technologies and motivated by the need for trained PM personnel capable of handling complex projects.	Shifting training from mirroring PM Body of Knowledge toward reflective and adaptive pedagogic system	(Christian and Soderlund, 2008; Francesca et al., 2016; Thomas and Mengel, 2008)

Health care	Complex and consists of multiple stakeholders (patients, hospitals, insurance, state and federal organizations, preexisting condition, individual and employers' mandates, Medicaid expansion, etc.)	The integration of PM temporality and organization permanent functions. Deep understanding of stakeholders' interests	(Batkins and Brannon, 2014; Boardman et al., 2016; Venkatesh et al., 2014; Godenhjelm et al, 2014)
IT	The field is ubiquitous and sine qua non-to organization success. It helps an organization provide products and services faster with a competitive price.	The role of program, portfolio, and what infrastructure is required to implement complex operations	(Moyland et al., 2015; Stone et al., 2015; Wagner et al., 2014; Wiener et al., 2016)

Management	Public and private organizations are increasingly integrating PPGE-based concepts.	Understanding PPGE-based organizations.	(Battistuzzo and Piscopo, 2015; Lu et al., 2015).
Pharmaceutics	Complex, nonlinear, and uncertain due to rising cost, regulation, socioeconomic and competitive pressures, lawsuits, mergers, restructuring, recalls, due to PPGE	Schedule, cost, and quality. Knowledge and innovation are required to understand the complexity and attain competitiveness	(Miterev et al., 2015; Kaiser et al., 2014; Rijke et al., 2014; Miterev et al., 2015; Herman and Handayani, 2015)
Transportation	The nature is complex, uncertain, chaotic, and nonlinear.	How to mobilize scarce resources to handle complex uncertainties and achieve competitive edge.	(Love et al., 2016); Nguyen et al., 2014; Qureshi and Kang, 2014; Sciara et al., 2016; Wilman, 2016)

Appendix O
Learning Curve

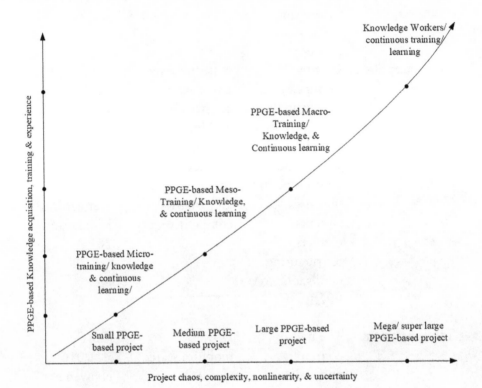

ABOUT THE AUTHOR

Dr. Abu Fofana provides thought-provoking and game-changing ideas that have helped business and project management leaders deliver business and project services when customers' demands require them. These complex projects are often mismanaged and fraught with a superficial understanding of the environmental and cultural differences, cost estimate errors, project cancellations, grafts, delays, and increasing stakeholder dissatisfactions worldwide.

Dr. Abu Mohammed Fofana has written numerous articles, including Practical Application of Project Management Theory, The Effects of Learning Curve on Your Project, Development of A Code of Ethics: Information Technology Challenges, How to Mitigate the Future Risks of a Project, How a Thorough Project Plan Assists an Effective Project Execution, Contrasting Project Portfolio Management, and Multiple Projects Project Control Process Evaluation.

Dr. Fofana is a founder of the Project Management Solution University and its prestigious PMSU Research Institute dedicated to researching and training the next generation of PM leaders poised and capable of taking on the challenges beyond the 20th First Century.

He served as a judge of the PMO Global Alliance Global Awards 2018 and 2019. In 2019, the PMO world body nominated Dr. Fofana for the prestigious PMO influencer award. He is an inducted member of the National Society of Leadership and Success. He lives in East Orange, New Jersey, United States.

CPSIA information can be obtained
at www.ICGtesting.com
Printed in the USA
BVHW080802231121
622259BV00003B/161